The Informal Economy

The Economy | Key Ideas

These short primers introduce students to the core concepts, theories and models, both new and established, heterodox and mainstream, contested and accepted, used by economists and political economists to understand and explain the workings of the economy.

Published

Behavioural Economics
Graham Mallard

Degrowth
Giorgos Kallis

The Informal Economy
Colin C. Williams

The Living Wage
Donald Hirsch and Laura Valadez-Martinez

Marginalism
Bert Mosselmans

The Resource Curse
S. Mansoob Murshed

The Informal Economy

Colin C. Williams

agenda
publishing

First published in 2019 by Agenda Publishing

Agenda Publishing Limited
The Core
Bath Lane
Newcastle Helix
Newcastle upon Tyne
NE4 5TF
www.agendapub.com

ISBN 978-1-911116-30-1 (hardcover)
ISBN 978-1-911116-31-8 (paperback)

British Library Cataloguing-in-Publication Data
A catalogue record for this book is available from the British Library

Typeset by JS Typesetting Ltd, Porthcawl, Mid Glamorgan
Printed and bound in the UK by TJ International

Contents

1

Defining the informal economy

Introduction

What is the informal economy? Why is it important to study? And what needs to be known about this sphere? The aim of this opening chapter is to answer these three key questions. In the first section, the various nouns and adjectives used to denote this sphere are reviewed along with the different definitions that have been used. The second section then reviews why it is important to study. To address this, it is necessary to consider the reasons from the perspective of not only informal workers and businesses, but also formal enterprises and workers, consumers as well as governments and societies. This will show that the negative consequences far outweigh any positive implications. The third and final section of this chapter then outlines the structure and argument of the book. At the outset, however, it is necessary to define the type of activity being discussed in this book.

What is the informal economy?

Ever since Keith Hart (1973) first introduced the concept of the "informal economy" in his study of Ghana nearly half a century ago, there has been an ongoing debate about how to define this sphere of economic activity and differentiate it from the formal economy. Indeed, what is here referred to as the "informal economy" has been alternatively denoted using over 45 different adjectives and 10 different nouns. It has been variously called the "black", "cash-in-hand", "hidden", "irregular", "invisible", "shadow", "subterranean", "undeclared", "underground", "unobserved", "unorganized" or "unregulated" economy, sector, work, employment, activity, sphere or realm, to name but a few.

Casting one's eyes over these adjectives, it becomes quickly apparent that all describe in various ways what is missing, insufficient or lacking about activity in the informal economy compared with activity in the formal economy (e.g. it is unorganized, unregulated or undeclared). Indeed, this is also a feature of all definitions of the informal economy. Reviewing the different types of definition used, three broad kinds can be identified, namely enterprise-, jobs- and activity-based definitions. Enterprise-based definitions describe what is absent, insufficient or lacking in informal economy enterprises compared with formal enterprises, jobs-based definitions what is absent, insufficient or lacking in informal jobs relative to formal jobs, and activity-based definitions what is absent, insufficient or lacking in informal economic activities compared with formal economic activities.

Starting with the enterprise-based definitions, in 1993 at the Fifteenth International Conference of Labour Statisticians (15th ICLS), a concerted effort was made to solve the various ambiguities in meaning that had emerged over the previous two decades since Hart had first introduced the concept (Hart 1973). To do so, employment in the informal sector was defined as comprising "all jobs in informal sector enterprises, or all persons who, during a given reference period, were employed in at least one informal sector enterprise, irrespective of their status of employment and whether it was their main or a secondary job" (Hussmanns 2005: 3). An informal sector enterprise was defined as a small or unregistered private unincorporated enterprise (Hussmanns 2005). Here, "small" refers to whether the numbers employed in the enterprise are below a specific threshold, determined according to national circumstances. An enterprise is "unregistered" in this ICLS definition if it is not registered under specific forms of national-level legislation (e.g. factories' or commercial acts, tax or social security laws, professional groups' regulatory acts). A "private unincorporated" enterprise meanwhile, is one owned by an individual or household that is not constituted as a separate legal entity independent of its owner, and for which no complete accounts is available that would permit a financial separation of the production activities of the enterprise from the other activities of its owner (Hussmanns 2005; ILO 2012, 2013).

One common problem that arose when this enterprise-based definition was applied in practice was that all small enterprises were sometimes wrongly classified as informal enterprises. Another problem was that this enterprise-centred definition failed to recognize the existence of informal employment in formal enterprises (e.g. formal businesses employing unregistered workers). In consequence, the Seventeenth ICLS in 2003 complemented this enterprise-based definition with a job-based definition of the informal economy. This included informal employment not only in informal enterprises but also in formal enterprises. In this job-based definition, "informal employment" includes all jobs included in the enterprise-centred definition of "employment in the informal sector" except those classified as formal jobs in informal sector enterprises, and "refers to those jobs that generally lack basic social or legal protections or employment benefits and may be found in the formal sector, informal sector or households" (ILO 2012: 12).

This job-based definition therefore recognizes that informal jobs exist in both informal and formal production units and that formal enterprises sometimes employ informal workers (Hussmanns 2005). It also covers both employers and own-account workers who are self-employed in their own informal sector enterprises, and contributing family workers and members of informal producers' cooperatives, as well as employees whose employment relationship is, in law or in practice, not subject to national labour legislation, income taxation, social protection or entitlement to certain employment benefits, such as severance pay, notice of dismissal, and annual paid leave or sick leave (Hussmanns 2005; ILO 2012, 2013; Williams & Lansky 2013).

Whilst these enterprise- and job-based definitions have dominated studies in the developing world, this has not been the case in relation to studies of the informal economy in the advanced economies and post-socialist transition societies. In part, this is because these definitions view enterprises and jobs dichotomously as either informal or formal. An enterprise is considered either formal or informal, and a job either formal or informal. This is perhaps relevant in the developing world but is less the case in developed and transition economies where it has become widely recognized that an enterprise and job can be concurrently both formal and informal. On the one hand, it is widely recognized in developed countries and transition economies that a considerable proportion of formal enterprises undertake a portion of their work in the informal economy such as under-reporting their income for tax purposes (Small Business Council 2004; Williams 2006a, 2010b). On the other hand, it is also recognized that many formal employees receive from formal employers part of their wage as a declared salary and part cash-in-hand as an undeclared ("envelope") salary (Horodnic 2016; Karpuskiene

2007; Meriküll & Staehr 2010; Neef 2002; Sedlenieks 2003; Williams 2010a, 2012a, 2012b, 2013a, 2013b; Williams & Horodnic 2017; Woolfson 2007; Žabko & Rajevska 2007). These prominent types of informality in developed countries and transition economies are not included in the enterprise-based definition since this work is in a formal enterprise or in the job-based definition since the worker is in a formal job (Hussmanns 2005).

Due to the differing character of the informal economy in developed and transition economies, therefore, the tendency has been to adopt an activity-based definition of the informal economy (Eurofound 2013; European Commission 1998, 2007; Sepulveda & Syrett 2007; Thomas 1992; Vanderseypen *et al.* 2013; Williams 2006b; Williams & Windebank 1998). The most frequently adopted activity-based definition is that published in 2002 by the Organisation for Economic Cooperation and Development (OECD), International Monetary Fund (IMF), International Labour Organization (ILO) and Interstate Statistical Committee of the Commonwealth of Independent States (CIS STAT) as a supplement to the System of National Accounts (SNA) 1993. This defines "underground production" (or what is here termed the "informal economy") as:

> all legal production activities that are deliberately concealed from public authorities ...: to avoid payment of income, value added or other taxes; to avoid payment of social security contributions; to avoid having to meet certain legal standards such as minimum wages, maximum hours, safety or health standards, etc. ...
> (OECD 2002: 139)

What is therefore absent, insufficient or lacking about the informal economy in this activity-based definition is that the activity is not declared to, hidden from, or unregistered with, the authorities for tax, social security and/or labour law purposes when it should be declared (Williams & Windebank 1998).

Other activity-based definitions of the informal economy used in developed and transition countries align closely with this OECD definition. For example, Schneider *et al.* (2010) similarly define what they term the "shadow" economy as all market-based legal production of goods and services that are deliberately concealed from public authorities to avoid either payment of taxes, social security contributions or legal labour market standards (e.g.

minimum wages, maximum working hours, safety standards). Likewise, although the European Commission has no official definition of the informal economy, the most widely used definition in the European Union similarly defines what it terms "undeclared" work as "any paid activities that are lawful as regards their nature but not declared to the public authorities, taking into account the differences in the regulatory system of Member States" (European Commission 2007: 2).

Although some new to the topic of the informal economy might believe that this book is about drug dealers, pimps, and those selling stolen or counterfeit goods on market stalls, if the good and/or service which is being traded is illegal (e.g. drug-trafficking, selling stolen goods), then this activity is *separately* defined as part of the wider "criminal" economy. It is a misnomer to think that what takes place in the wider illegal or criminal economy (see Friman 2004) is the same as the informal economy. The goods and/or services traded in the informal economy are legal. Therefore, this criminal activity where illegal goods and/or services are traded is not covered in this book. Similarly, if the activity is unpaid, it is not part of the informal economy but rather, part of the unpaid subsistence economy. Nevertheless, as always, there is some blurring of the boundaries between these realms, for example, whether a good and/or service traded is legal or illegal and therefore whether it is part of the informal economy or wider criminal economy, will vary: a good or service in some countries is legal in others (e.g. cannabis, prostitution). Similarly, whether an activity is paid or unpaid can become blurred when activities are reimbursed in-kind using reciprocal labour and/or gifts instead of money. Typically, however, only paid activities are included when defining whether activities belong to the informal economy (Williams 2006a).

Throughout this book, an activity-based definition is adopted. The informal economy refers to activity that is legal in all respects other than it is not declared to, hidden from, or unregistered with, the authorities for tax, social security and/or labour law purposes when it should be declared. However, this does not mean that such activity is *unregulated*. This is a common mistake. As Castells and Portes (1989: 15) erroneously assert, the informal economy is "a specific form of income generating production … unregulated by the institutions of society in a legal and social environment in which similar activities are regulated". Although these commentators valuably view the informal sector through the lens of the institutions of society, they fail to distinguish how informal activities are viewed differently by the "legal" (formal) institutions and "social" (informal) institutions in a society. Viewed from an institutional theory perspective (Baumol & Blinder 2008; North 1990), all societies have both formal institutions (i.e. laws and regulations) that define the legal rules of the game, as well as informal institutions, which are the "socially shared rules, usually unwritten, that are created, communicated and enforced outside of officially sanctioned channels" (Helmke & Levitsky 2004: 727). The above definition fails to recognize first, that the informal economy, although unregulated by formal institutions, is regulated by the rules of informal institutions and secondly, that activity in the informal economy is considered "legitimate" from the viewpoint of informal institutions even if deemed "illegal" from the standpoint of the laws and regulations of the formal institutions (Siqueira *et al.* 2016; Webb *et al.* 2009; Williams *et al.* 2017).

The activity-based definition therefore requires a minor addition to bring clarity to whether the informal economy is regulated or not, as well as whether the activity is paid or not. As such, the activity-based definition adopted in this book is that the informal economy is *socially legitimate paid activity that is legal in all respects other than that it is not declared to, hidden from or unregistered with, the authorities for tax, social security and/ or labour law purposes when it should be declared.* If the activity is illegal in other respects and/or deemed socially illegitimate, then it is not part of the informal economy but instead part of the criminal economy (e.g. forced labour, selling stolen goods, trafficking illegal drugs) which is both illegal from the viewpoint of formal institutions and illegitimate from the viewpoint of informal institutions.

Why is the informal economy important to study?

To understand the importance of studying the informal economy, it is necessary to appreciate the consequences of its existence for the various groups affected by it, namely formal enterprises, informal businesses, informal workers, customers of the informal economy, governments, and the wider economy and society. Earlier scholarship on the informal economy focused near enough entirely upon its negative consequences (e.g. Castells & Portes 1989). Over the past two decades, however, a more balanced approach has begun to emerge. This recognizes that the informal economy can sometimes have potentially positive consequences. Here, in consequence, each group affected by the informal economy is examined in turn in terms of both its negative as well as positive consequences for them. At the outset, nevertheless, it should be stated that the widespread consensus is that the negative consequences are far greater than the positive consequences.

Formal businesses

For formal businesses, the informal economy represents unfair competition. Enterprises operating in the informal economy have an unfair competitive advantage over formal businesses since they do not abide by the labour laws, often ignore health and safety legislation, and evade tax and social insurance payments (Andrews *et al.* 2011; Bajada & Schneider 2005; Evans *et al.* 2006; Grabiner 2000; Karlinger 2013; Renooy *et al.* 2004; Small Business Council 2004). They therefore have lower production costs and can undercut formal businesses. Indeed, when these informal enterprises start to have a major impact on the development and growth of formal businesses, then the formal businesses may themselves begin to question whether they should any longer conform to the legal "rules of the game". The outcome is further informalization due to formal businesses starting to operate partially or fully in the informal economy, and businesses that already conduct a portion of their trade in the informal economy undertaking an even greater proportion undeclared (Gallin 2001; Grabiner 2000; Mateman & Renooy 2001; Small Business Council 2004; Williams & Windebank 1998). This results in a vicious downward spiral whereby ever greater proportions of trade take place in the informal economy.

The consequences for businesses of the informal economy, however, are not necessarily universally negative. One potentially positive consequence is that the informal economy can act as an incubator for business start-ups where they "test-trade" to see whether the venture is viable before taking a decision on whether to create a fully formal and legitimate business venture (Williams & Martinez 2014a). In the UK, for example, one-fifth of existing formal businesses report that they test-traded in the informal economy before registering and legitimizing their business (Williams & Martinez 2014c). Autio and Fu (2015) further reinforce this finding in a wider context, revealing that across the globe, two-thirds of businesses start-up in the informal economy without registration. This is the case not only in developing and transition countries (where 0.62 unregistered businesses are created annually for every 100 people, compared with 0.37 registered businesses) but also in OECD countries (where 0.62 unregistered businesses compared with 0.43 registered businesses are annually created for every 100 people).

A further positive consequence, which is specific to the developing world, is that formal businesses that started-up unregistered display higher subsequent rates of employment, sales and productivity growth compared with businesses that started-up registered and fully legitimate. This is because these enterprises that initially avoided the cost of registration and focused their resources on overcoming other liabilities of newness, established a stronger foundation for subsequent growth than those that registered from the outset (Williams *et al.* 2017). The benefits of formalization in the developing world are often insufficient to outweigh the potential costs of initially operating in the informal economy (Williams & Kedir 2017a, 2017b).

A further advantage of the informal economy, particularly for larger formal businesses, is that flexible production and cost reduction can be achieved by sub-contracting and outsourcing to informal workers and businesses (Castells & Portes 1989; Davis 2006; Gallin 2001; Hudson 2005; Meagher 2010; Slavnic 2010; Taiwo 2013). The informal economy is often an integral component of the supply chains of formal businesses because outsourcing and sub-contracting to informal businesses and workers is cheaper than doing so to formal businesses (Ketchen *et al.* 2014) and is commonly used by formal enterprises to reduce their production and distribution costs (Castells & Portes 1989; Meagher 2010).

Informal sector businesses

The consequences for informal businesses can be again both negative and positive. Starting with the negative consequences, businesses and sole traders operating in the informal economy find that their opportunities to develop and grow their business are severely constrained for at least five reasons:

1. They are often unable to gain access to finance capital to develop their business since they have no formal accounts (ILO 2015; Kempson 1996; Leonard 1994; Llanes & Barbour 2007);

2. They cannot advertise their business openly to attract new customers for fear of being detected by the authorities (Williams *et al.* 2012a);
3. They need to keep their business small to stay "under the radar" of the authorities (Barbour & Llanes 2013; Williams *et al.* 2012a);
4. They cannot secure formal intellectual property rights to their process and product innovations (De Beer *et al.* 2013); and
5. They lack access to business support compared with formal businesses to help them develop and grow (ILO 2002; Karjanen 2014; Llanes & Barbour 2007; Williams & Nadin, 2013a, 2013b, 2014).

The informal economy, however, also has some potentially positive consequences for businesses and sole traders in the informal economy:

1. It provides a source of income, a survival strategy and a means of livelihood for people excluded from the formal economy, by providing opportunities for "necessity-driven entrepreneurship" (Williams & Shahid 2015);
2. It can reduce the barriers to entry into work because most work in the informal economy is purportedly either labour-intensive production requiring few skills and little start-up capital in developing countries, or starts with close social relations in developed nations (Chen 2012; Williams & Lansky 2013);
3. It provides an exit strategy in contexts where the regulatory burden stifles business development (De Soto 1989, 2001);
4. It provides businesses and sole traders with an escape route from the corrupt practices of public sector officials who would demand bribes if the businesses sought to operate in the formal economy (Round *et al.* 2008; Tonoyan *et al.* 2010); and
5. It arguably provides greater flexibility in where, when and how to work, especially important for women who remain responsible for child-care (Chen 2012; Snyder 2004).

Informal workers

For those employed as workers in the informal economy, there are similarly both negative and positive consequences. The negative consequences of being in dependent waged employment in the informal economy are ten-fold. Informal workers:

1. Do not have automatic access to standard employment rights such as annual and other leave, sickness and redundancy pay, and training (Evans *et al.* 2006; ILO 2015; TUC 2008; Williams & Lansky 2013);
2. Lack access to a range of other legal rights such as the minimum wage, tax credits and any working hours directives (Dellot 2012; Renooy *et al.* 2004; TUC 2008; Vanderseypen *et al.* 2013; Williams & Windebank 1998);
3. Cannot accrue rights to a state pension and other contributory benefits, and access occupational pension schemes (Dellot 2012; Gallin 2001; ILO 2002; Williams & Lansky 2013);
4. Lack access to health and safety standards in the workplace (Evans *et al.* 2006; Gallin 2001; ILO 2002, 2015; TUC 2008);
5. Have lower job security compared with formal employees (Katungi *et al.* 2006; Kovács 2014; Williams 2001);
6. Lack collective bargaining rights (ILO 2002, 2014);
7. Lose employability due to their lack of evidence of prior engagement in employment (Barbour & Llanes 2013; Dellot 2012);
8. Are unable to gain access to credit such as mortgages or loans since they have no evidence of their income (Kempson 1996; Williams 2014d);
9. Are unable to get an employer's reference (ILO 2002; TUC 2008); and
10. Suffer a constant fear of detection (Grabiner 2000).

The positive consequences of working in the informal economy for waged employees meanwhile, are that it provides them with a source of income in circumstances when other means of livelihood and/or social protection may not be available to them, and some flexibility regarding where, when and how they work. However, the negative consequences appear to largely outweigh the positive consequences for waged employees in the informal economy.

Informal economy customers

Another group, sometimes forgotten when considering the consequences of the informal economy, are the *customers* who purchase goods and services in this realm. Again, there are both negative and positive consequences. The negative consequences for customers who purchase goods and services in the informal economy are that:

- They may find it more difficult to take legal action if the work undertaken is of a quality that is poor, inadequate or insufficient (Eurofound 2013; Small Business Council 2004);
- Their insurance cover is invalid (Llanes & Barbour 2007; Small Business Council 2004);
- They have no guarantees in relation to the quality of the work undertaken (Williams *et al.* 2012a);
- There is no certainty that there has been adherence to health and safety regulations (Dellot 2012; Williams *et al.* 2012a); and
- Despite the assumption that goods and services purchased in the informal economy are cheaper, this might not always be the case. Informal enterprises operating in various "bottom of the pyramid" markets are often hugely inefficient and as such, unlikely to be able to charge lower prices for the same products (London *et al.* 2014).

Whether this latter point is the case is of course open to debate and, similar to other claims regarding the positive and negative consequences of the informal economy, there is currently little empirical evidence available.

Turning to the positive consequences for consumers, other commentators have indeed claimed that the informal economy provides purchasers with more affordable goods and services not only in low-income environments such as "bottom of the pyramid" (BOP) markets (Ketchen *et al.* 2014) but also in higher-income economies when payment is made in cash and no receipts change hands (Williams 2014a; Williams & Martinez 2014b; Williams *et al.* 2012b).

Economies and societies

There are also consequences for the wider economies and societies in which work in the informal economy takes place. The negative consequences for the broader economy and society are that:

- Although informal businesses are supposedly low-productivity enterprises and lack the scale to produce efficiently, they gain substantial cost advantages by avoiding taxes and regulations, which offsets their low productivity and small scale. However, they reduce the overall level of productivity in economies and hinder the development of higher productivity economies, thus impeding overall economic development and growth (La Porta & Schleifer 2008, 2014; Williams 2014a);

- The existence of an informal economy can have knock-on effects on the rule of law and encourage a more casual attitude to the law more widely (Gallin 2001; Grabiner 2000; Mateman & Renooy 2001; Small Business Council 2004; Williams & Windebank 1998); and
- Informal economies result in weakened trade union and collective bargaining (Gallin 2001; TUC 2008).

Reviewing the potential positive consequences of the informal economy for wider societies and economies, meanwhile, it can be asserted that the informal economy:

- Provides employment and work, even if it is unregistered employment (Ketchen *et al.* 2014);
- Provides a breeding ground for the micro-enterprise system and test-bed for fledgling businesses and thus facilitates the development of entrepreneurship and an enterprise culture (Williams & Martinez-Perez 2014a); and
- Enables income (earned in the informal economy) to be spent in the formal economy which boosts demand for formal goods and services and contributes to official economic growth (Schneider & Williams 2013).

Governments

Finally, and for governments, the consequences of the informal economy are again both negative and positive. The negative consequences of the informal economy are:

- A loss of revenue for the state in terms of non-payment of direct and indirect taxes (Bajada & Schneider 2005; Evans *et al.* 2006; Grabiner

2000; Müller & Miggelbrink 2014; Vanderseypen *et al.* 2013; Williams & Windebank 1998);
- Knock-on effects on efforts to forge social cohesion at a societal level by reducing the money available to governments to pursue social integration and mobility initiatives (Andrews *et al.* 2011; Eurofound 2013; Vanderseypen *et al.* 2013);
- A loss of regulatory control over the quality of jobs and services provided in the economy (ILO 2013; Vanderseypen *et al.* 2013; Williams & Lansky 2013), and
- An attitude amongst participants that the law more widely does not have to be obeyed (Andrews *et al.* 2011; Dong *et al.* 2012; Karjanen 2014; Morris & Polese 2014; Ojo *et al.* 2013; Sasunkevich 2014).

The positive consequences of the informal economy for governments, at least in the eyes of some commentators, are:

- It encourages governments from introducing burdensome regulatory regimes because if they do, then businesses will move into the informal economy to avoid the burdensome costs and regulations involved (De Soto 1989, 2001); and
- Any "on the job" training in informal businesses alleviates pressure on the state and its agencies to provide training, especially in times of reduced public spending (Williams 2014a).

In sum, the informal economy is important to study not for one individual reason but for many reasons. It has significant consequences for formal businesses, informal enterprises, informal employees, customers who purchase goods and services in the informal economy, the wider economy and society, and governments. Although most of these consequences have not been enumerated to measure the actual impacts of the informal economy, there is little doubt that the informal economy has important consequences. Neither, moreover, is there much doubt that if these consequences were to be enumerated, then the negative consequences would outweigh the positive consequences. It can be stated, therefore, that the informal economy is important to study, but that the reasons it is important depend on the stakeholder, and that the net effect of the informal economy (for stakeholders taken as a whole) is deleterious. Given this, attention turns to the structure of the rest of the book which seeks to understand not only the extent, character and determinants of the informal economy but also what should be done to tackle it.

Structure and argument of the book

What different theories have been used to explain the informal economy and how have the dominant theoretical explanations changed over time? How can the informal economy be measured and what is its size? What types of informal work exist, who does it and what are their motives for participating in the informal economy? And what policy options are available for tackling the informal economy? What is the current approach being pursued and why, and what alternative policy approaches and measures might be used instead to tackle the informal economy?

This book addresses each of these questions in turn. In Chapter 2, the different theories used to explain the informal economy are reviewed along with how the dominant theoretical explanations have changed over time. This reveals that modernization theory, which viewed the informal economy as a leftover from a pre-modern economic system and one slowly disappearing as economies modernized, dominated for most of the twentieth century. From this perspective, therefore, the informal economy persists only due to economic underdevelopment and a lack of modernization of governance. However, the recognition that the informal economy is a continuously prevailing feature of contemporary economies has led to the emergence of alternative perspectives. On the one hand, a political economy perspective has viewed the informal economy as an inherent feature of contemporary capitalism that is growing, if anything, as firms outsource and sub-contract production to informal workers and enterprises, with workers pushed into the informal economy to survive. From this perspective, therefore, the informal economy persists due to inadequate state intervention in work and welfare, and a lack of protection of workers. On the other hand, and conversely, a neoliberal perspective maintains the informal economy to result from over-regulation of the economy, such as high taxes and burdensome regulations and controls, and thus depicts workers and businesses as voluntarily exiting the formal economy. However, none of these theories, each of which focus upon various national-level structural determinants, has been able to explain why some workers and businesses in a particular context turn to the informal economy and why others do not. Chapter 2 thus concludes by examining how institutional theory has been used to explain this irregularity.

Chapter 3 then turns its attention to evaluating the magnitude of the informal economy. This will briefly review the various measurement methods used to estimate the size of the informal economy and provide estimates of its varying size across the globe. Building on Chapter 2, it will also evaluate the validity of the various theories by examining whether cross-national variations in the size of the informal economy are indeed correlated with economic underdevelopment and a lack of modernization of governance (modernization theory), too little state intervention in work and welfare (political economy theory), state over-interference in the form of high taxes and burdensome regulation (neoliberal theory) and the relevance of institutional theory.

Chapter 4 then turns its attention to the character of the informal economy. This will review the different varieties of work in the informal economy, who does it and why they do it. One major outcome will be to identify the existence of a lower tier of necessity-driven informal workers and an upper-tier of informal workers who engage in the informal economy more out of choice.

Having reviewed and evaluated the different explanations for the informal economy, its varying size and its characteristics, Chapter 5 then turns its attention to what is to be done about the informal economy. This will review the different policy options available to governments. Chapter 6 then concludes the book by synthesizing the findings and discussing future directions for the study of the informal economy. In doing so, the hope is that this book will contribute significantly to the advancement of understanding regarding not only the extent and character of the informal economy but also, perhaps more importantly, to what needs to be done to tackle this persistent and extensive sphere that dominates the global economic landscape.

2

Theories explaining the informal economy

Introduction

The aim of this chapter is to review the major competing theories of the informal economy, namely: modernization theory, which argues that economic underdevelopment and unmodern systems of governance cause large informal economies; neoliberal theory, which asserts that too much government intervention (e.g. high taxes, burdensome regulations and controls) is the cause; and political economy theory, which conversely argues that inadequate state intervention and the lack of protection of workers are the causes. This is followed by a review of institutional theory which asserts that formal institutional failures lead to an asymmetry between formal rules, and informal norms, values and beliefs, resulting in greater prevalence of the informal economy.

Modernization theory

Over the course of the twentieth century, modernization theory was the dominant explanation for large informal economies. In this theory, the informal economy is part of the pre-modern economic system and its presence in economies will reduce as the modern formal economy becomes established (Geertz 1963; Gilbert 1998; Lewis 1959; Packard 2007). As Ray Bromley (2007: xv) explains, the informal economy from this perspective is "unimportant and destined to disappear" with economic development and the modernization of governance. Sometimes referred to as "residue" or "dual economy" theory, the informal economy is portrayed as a leftover from an earlier economic system which is disappearing with economic development and modernization.

This dualistic representation of the economy as composed of discrete formal and informal economies is associated with scholars such as Julius Boeke (1942) in relation to his studies on South-East Asia, and the economist Arthur Lewis (1954). The depiction of the formal and informal economies as dualistic opposites differed to the then dominant neoclassical economic models, although Lewis was in that tradition. At the core of the dualist view was the view that less developed countries had two different sectors. One was capitalist, modern, progressive, dynamic and depicted as capital-intensive. The other, the "subsistence" or "peasant" sector (or in later terminology the "marginal" sector) was pre-capitalist, reliant on family labour, unsophisticated in its production and operations, used low technology and possessed poor productivity. For Lewis (1954), economic development involved the absorption and transformation of the latter sector into the former. Boeke (1942), meanwhile, developing the notion of "social dualism", maintained a culture clash to exist between the imported social system (e.g., capitalism) and the indigenous social system of the informal economy, thus viewing them not only as discrete economic systems but also as separate social systems incorporating different social values. He did not believe that the two separate systems could successfully coexist and so believed it was necessary to "transform" the traditional pre-capitalist system into a "modern" one.

In broader philosophical terms, this "dual economy" depiction of the formal and informal economies in modernization theory is akin to the theory of binary oppositions outlined by Jacques Derrida (1967). For him, western ideas are based on binary thinking whereby activity is viewed in either/or terms as discrete binary opposites. In his thesis of hierarchical binary thought, Derrida suggests that these either/or opposites are ordered in a hierarchical normative manner and a temporal sequencing with each other – one binary opposite is considered superordinate, while the other is subordinate. In modernization theory, this is clearly seen. The informal economy is subordinate, negative, associated with underdevelopment, and declining. The formal economy, meanwhile, is superordinate, positive, connected with progress, and growing (Williams & Round 2008; Williams 2014a).

In temporal terms, therefore, modernization theory views the superordinate formal economy as growing and replacing the dwindling subordinate informal economy. In the middle of the last century, for example, the widespread belief was that industrialization, economic development and modernization would pull workers in developing countries out of the supposedly unproductive informal economy and into the modern industrial formal economy. This theory stemmed from the experience of rebuilding Europe and Japan following the Second World War, and the expansion of industrialization in the United States and the UK. The assumption was that a mono-dimensional linear pattern of economic development exists in which less developed countries, naturally and inevitably, follow the path of capitalist economic development "enjoyed" by the advanced economies.

This perceived linear trajectory of economic development thus lead to countries being classified by their relative level of economic advancement and modernization, and they were placed in a development queue with nations at the fore with small informal economies being "advanced", "modern" and "progressive", and nations at the back of the queue with large informal economies being deemed "backward", "traditional" and "underdeveloped" (Geertz 1963; Gilbert 1998; Lewis 1959; Packard 2007).

This perception of a one-dimensional linear development path for all countries, however, takes no account of their different histories, and that the global economic and political situation facing Africa, Asia and Latin America was very different from that experienced by Europe and North America. Neither is it considered that global power relations are skewed in favour of those already "modern" advanced economies. Indeed, one of the main reasons for the refutation of modernization theory in the last two decades or so is "a widespread recognition that the informal sector is not some weak and disappearing realm but strong, persistent and even growing in the contemporary global economy" (Williams & Round 2007a: 32).

In normative terms, moreover, the superordinate formal economy is depicted as virtuous, positive and beneficial. Meanwhile, the informal economy is seen as harmful, negative and deleterious. However, it is not just the temporal and normative hierarchical sequencing of the formal and informal economy in modernization theory that is important. Deborah Potts (2008) argues that the erroneous depiction of "disconnection" between the two sectors is important. She argues that this modernization perspective "has descriptive value but is dangerously misleading if translated into policy that is founded on an idea that the sectors are functionally separate" (Potts 2008: 152–3).

In much contemporary literature on the informal economy, this modernization theory is often portrayed as an old theoretical perspective that has been superseded. This is largely because of its view that the subordinate informal economy is declining and fading from view as economies develop and modernize their governance. However, in recent years, modernization theory, albeit in an updated form, has re-emerged. Rafael La Porta and Andrei Shleifer (2008, 2014) recognize the persistence of informality and its extensiveness, but nonetheless continue to portray the informal and formal economies as disconnected sectors and the informal economy as normatively negative, depicting informal workers as typically uneducated people operating small unproductive enterprises in separate "bottom of the pyramid" (BOP) markets producing low-quality products for low-income consumers using little capital and adding little value. The core tenets of modernization theory are therefore maintained: that the formal and informal economies are a hierarchical binary, with the formal economy endowed with positive features and the informal economy with negative features. So too is the view that the prevalence of the informal economy is associated with the level of economic development and quality of governance and corruption.

Political economy theory

The recognition that the informal economy is not declining has resulted in a body of scholarship that adopts a political economy perspective viewing the formal and informal economies as intertwined. Propagated by Caroline Moser in the late 1970s (Moser 1977) and by Alejandro Portes, Manuel Castells and colleagues in the late 1980s (see Castells & Portes 1989; Portes 1994), this rejects the depiction of the informal economy as a residue of traditional economic systems (i.e., economic dualism). Instead, those in the informal economy are viewed as working in subordinate economic units and a view is adopted of the structural dependency of the informal economy and the exploitation of the informal workforce by the formal economy (Castells & Portes 1989). The two economies are therefore seen as functionally related sectors and part of the same economic system, namely late capitalism (Portes 1994).

For those writing from this political economy perspective, the growth of the informal economy is a direct by-product of the emergence of an ever more deregulated and open world economy (Aliyev 2015; Bhattacharya 2014; Dibben & Williams 2012; Dibben *et al.* 2015; Gallin 2001; Harriss-White

2014; Hudson 2005; Sassen 1996). The increasing functional integration of a single global economic system results in sub-contracting and outsourcing becoming a primary means of integrating employment in the informal economy into contemporary capitalism, causing a downward pressure on wages and the erosion of incomes, social services and benefits, and the growth of yet more jobs in the informal economy. As Patricia Fernandez-Kelly (2006: 18) states, "the informal sector is far from a vestige of earlier stages in economic development. Instead, informality is part and parcel of the processes of modernization". For example, this can be clearly seen in how workers who were former employees now engage in "bogus self-employment" for one supplier in the so-called "gig" or "platform" economy in order that the "employer" can evade paying tax and social security contributions (Williams & Lapeyre 2017). Indeed, for Mike Davis (2006: 186), such "primitive forms of exploitation ... have been given new life by postmodern globalization". Informal work is integrated into contemporary capitalism to reduce production costs (Castells & Portes 1989; Davis 2006; Meagher 2010; Slack *et al.* 2017; Slavnic 2010; Taiwo 2013).

The growth of the informal economy, therefore, is part of what Michael Piore and Charles Sabel (1984) describe as a reorganization of production into small-scale, decentralized and more flexible economic units, associated with the shift away from Fordist mass production and towards "flexible specialisation". The outcome is an informalization of employment relations. Standard wage jobs (i.e., regular full-time jobs) are turned into non-standard wage jobs (including part-time, temporary and contract jobs) with hourly wages but few benefits, or into piece-rate jobs with no benefits, self-employment expands, and production of goods and services is sub-contracted to small-scale informal units and outworkers. As such, the informal economy becomes a permanent, but subordinate and dependent, feature of modern capitalist development.

Meanwhile, structural adjustment in Africa and economic transition in the former Soviet Union and in Central and Eastern Europe are also associated with an expansion of the informal economy. This is because, in response to global competition, formal firms hire all but a few core workers under informal arrangements or outsource the production of goods and services to other firms and countries. Informality, therefore, is not simply an outcome of excess labour supply or over-regulation (Yusuff 2011: 628). Instead, the informal economy "exists to serve the needs of the larger firms by supplying cheaper goods and services" (Dellot 2012: 16). As a result, the "rich formal sector extracts value from the poor informal sector" (Godfrey 2011: 246).

Moreover, the resultant diminishing state involvement in social protection and economic intervention accompanying deregulation are seen to lead those excluded from the formal labour market and social protection to be pushed into the informal economy as a survival strategy (Chen 2012; ILO 2014; Meagher 2010; Mešić 2016; Sasaki *et al.* 2016; Taiwo 2013). Consequently, although recognizing informal work as intertwined with the formal economy, it remains depicted as having negative impacts. First, this is because economies are viewed as losing "natural" competitiveness because productive formal enterprises suffer unfair competition from these informal economic units (Leal Ordóñez 2014; Levy 2008; Lewis 2004). Secondly, governments are viewed as losing both regulatory control over work conditions (ILO 2014) and tax revenue (Bajada & Schneider 2005), and thirdly, customers as lacking legal recourse and certainty that health and safety regulations have been followed (Williams & Martinez-Perez 2014e).

Informal workers are consequently viewed by political economy scholars as low-paid marginalized populations participating in such work out of necessity, as a survival strategy, in the absence of alternative means of livelihood (e.g. Barsoum 2015; Castells & Portes 1989; Gallin 2001; Lagos 1995; Maldonado 1995). As Andrew Travers (2002: 2) puts it, "It is usually said that people do the work to earn extra money and left at that". From studies of street-sellers in the Dominican Republic (e.g. Itzigsohn 2000), China (Lin 2018), Nepal (Karki & Xheneti 2018), South Africa (Petersen & Charman 2018), Latin American cities (Linares 2018) and Somalia (Little 2003), through studies of informal garment businesses in India (e.g., Das 2003; Unai & Rani 2003) and the Philippines (Doane *et al.* 2003), to studies of home-based workers in Mexico (e.g., Staudt 1998) and Martinique (Browne 2004) and waste-pickers in the global South (Coletto & Bisschop 2017), this is depicted as work conducted out of necessity as a survival strategy (e.g., Itzigsohn 2000; Otero 1994; Rakowski 1994a). As Sharit Bhowmik (2005: 96) explains, for these marginalized populations, the informal economy "is the only means for survival". The characteristics of those active in the informal economy, as opposed to those in the formal, are quite specific and can be considered under the general heading of "downgraded labour" (Sassen 1996).

For political economy scholars, therefore, the informal economy results from low levels of state intervention in the economy and welfare, and a lack of protection of workers. The informal economy is consequently greater when taxes are lower, public expenditure as a proportion of GDP is lower, and there are lower levels of social protection. High taxes are thus not a cause of the informal economy. Rather, countries with high tax rates are argued to have lower levels of the informal economy, mostly because they have forged a social contract with their citizens that allows them to have higher levels of public expenditure via taxes to fund social protection programmes, such as welfare safety nets and active labour market policies that reduce the necessity of engaging in the informal economy as a survival practice (Williams & Horodnic 2015a, 2015b, 2015c).

Neoliberal theory

For neoliberal scholars, in stark contrast to political economy scholars, the informal economy is not so much a necessity-driven endeavour undertaken as a last resort, but more a matter of choice and a response to the over-regulation of the formal economy. It is a populist reaction to high taxes and too much interference in the free market. For these neoliberals, workers in the informal economy are throwing off the shackles of high taxes and an over-intrusive state (e.g. De Soto 1989; Sauvy 1984). It is a rational economic decision to participate in the informal economy since it enables them to escape the over-regulated formal economy (Becker 2004; De Soto 1989, 2001; London & Hart 2004; Nwabuzor 2005; Sauvy 1984; Schneider & Williams 2013). Workers thus voluntarily operate in the informal economy to avoid the financial costs of formal registration along with the associated time and effort required (De Soto 1989, 2001; Perry & Maloney 2007; Small Business Council 2004). As Augustine Nwabuzor (2005: 126) asserts, "Informality is a response to burdensome controls, and an attempt to circumvent them", or as Gary Becker (2004: 10) explains, "informal work arrangements are a rational response by micro-entrepreneurs to over-regulation by government bureaucracies".

A prominent advocate of this view has been Peruvian economist Hernando De Soto, whose central hypothesis is that the costs of formalization and over-regulation hinder entrepreneurs, and that deregulation and simplification of the registration procedure results in economic freedom and the flourishing of entrepreneurship in developing countries (De Soto 1989). For such neoliberal scholars, those currently operating in the informal economy could positively contribute to economic growth and development but cannot at present because they are constrained by state-imposed institutional constraints which support mercantilist interests (De Soto 1989: xix). The informal economy in this sense, is a revolutionary movement of free market enterprise against over-regulation. These workers wish to work formally but cannot do so due to the heavy costs of formalization and bureaucracy, which make it almost impossible to do so. Informal work is thus the people's "spontaneous and creative response to the state's incapacity to satisfy the basic needs of the impoverished masses" (De Soto 1989: xiv–v). It is a rational economic decision taken by those whose entrepreneurial spirit is stifled by high taxes and over-regulation (De Soto 1989, 2001; Perry & Maloney 2007; Small Business Council 2004).

Indeed, Saumyajit Bhattacharya (2014) contextualizes these neoliberal arguments regarding the informal economy by identifying seven waves of neoliberal anti-labour discourse. Sequentially, these have: (1) attacked labour "rigidities" rather than focused on labour's hard-won rights; (2) treated low-cost labour as a comparative advantage; (3) viewed labour rights as obstacles and luxuries; (4) adopted the doctrine and practice of flexibilization in advanced countries; (5) pursued the paradigm of informality and the gulfs between formal and informal labour in developing countries; (6) called to formalize informal workers and disguised the informalization of formal workers; and (7) celebrated enterprise culture and informal entrepreneurialism.

The recent wave of neoliberal scholars on the informal economy, in consequence, are more positive and celebratory of informal workers than either modernization theorists or political economy theorists. Informal workers are the vanguard of a popular movement against too much state intervention, and voluntarily decide to engage in such endeavour (Adom & Williams 2012a, 2012b, 2014; Cross 2000; Gerxhani 2004; Gurtoo & Williams 2009; Maloney 2004; Snyder 2004). For example, John Cross (2000) argues that although street vendors have been conventionally portrayed as necessity-driven, most of those he studied did so out of choice to avoid the costs, time and effort of formal registration (see also Cross & Morales 2007). In other words, the informal economy offers them potential benefits that they cannot find in the formal economy, including flexible hours, job training, opportunity for economic independence, better wages and the avoidance of taxes and inefficient government regulation (Maloney 2004).

The policy approach advocated, therefore, is to pursue tax reductions, reduce the "regulatory burden" and state over-interference. De Soto (1989) famously proposed that governments, and Peru's specifically, push firms into the informal sector by raising the barriers and costs of formalization. By excluding firms from the formal sector, these barriers stifle entrepreneurship and reduce the dynamism of the private sector. Others such as Santiago Levy (2008) have claimed that the high levels of informality display the propensity of small firms to escape from this over-burdensome system. This "exit" leads to a vicious cycle. Firms escape because the state does not make formalization appealing. For example, financial markets and courts may be dysfunctional, and public procurement processes may be corrupt. By being in the informal sector, firms avoid paying taxes that would provide resources the state might use to improve the provision of public goods. The result is that even more escape creating a spiral of informalization.

For neoliberal commentators (Loayza 2007; Schneider & Enste 2000; Schneider & Klinglmair 2004; Schneider *et al.* 2010), therefore, the main drivers of the informal economy are tax and social security contribution burdens (Cebula 1997; Feld & Schneider 2010; Friedman *et al.* 2000; Giles 1999; Giles & Tedds 2002; Hill & Kabir 1996; Johnson *et al.* 1998; Schneider 2005; Tanzi 1999) and the intensity of regulations, since it implies an increase in costs that discourages participation in the formal economy (Johnson *et al.* 1997). According to Friedrich Schneider and Robert Klinglmair (2004), "The bigger the difference between the total cost of labour in the formal sector and the after-tax earnings (from work), the greater is the incentive to avoid this difference". Given that this difference is broadly based on the social security and tax burdens, these are viewed as key causes of larger informal economies. For scholars such as Richard Cebula (1997), therefore, there is a need to reduce the tax burden (i.e., the amount of income, property or sales tax, levied on individuals or businesses, measured by the effective tax rate, which is the ratio of tax revenue to GDP). However, Johnson *et al.* (1998) and Schneider (2002) are more cautious. They argue that it is not higher tax rates that increase the size of the informal economy, but the ineffective and discretionary application of the tax system and regulations by governments.

Institutional theory

These three theorizations all propose structural causes of the informal econ-omy. As such, they do not explain why some citizens and businesses within a country participate in the informal economy and others do not. Since the turn of the millennium, this theoretical gap has been bridged by adopting the lens of institutional theory (Baumol & Blinder 2008; Helmke & Levitsky 2004; North 1990). Institutions are the rules of the game. Such rules exist in all societies and govern behaviour. As structures and mechanisms of social order, or governance mechanisms, institutions comprise governing laws, contracts, property rights, and other legal and operational codes (i.e., formal institutions), as well as prescribed norms, values and beliefs about what is acceptable (i.e. informal institutions). From the perspective of institutional theory, therefore, all societies have on the one hand, formal institutions (i.e. codified laws and regulations) that are the legal rules of the game, and on the other hand, informal institutions which are the unwritten socially shared rules existing outside of official codes and laws (Helmke & Levitsky 2004), and are the norms, values and beliefs held by citizens, workers and employers reflecting their individual ethics about what is right and accept-able (Denzau & North 1994).

Viewed through this institutionalist lens, economic activity in the for-mal economy adheres to the formal institutional prescriptions set out in the codified laws and regulations. Economic activity in the informal economy, in contrast, occurs outside of these formal institutional prescriptions but within the norms, values and beliefs of informal institutions (Godfrey 2011; Kistruck *et al.* 2015; Siqueira *et al.* 2016; Webb *et al.* 2009; Welter *et al.* 2015; Williams & Gurtoo 2017a). Criminal activity, meanwhile, occurs not only outside of formal institutional prescriptions but also outside the socially shared rules regarding what is acceptable.

Institutional theory has been used to explain the informal economy in three successive waves. Originally, in the first wave, it was explained as result-ing from formal institutional failures and imperfections, including formal institutional resource misallocations and inefficiencies, voids, weaknesses, and instability. Subsequently, in a second wave, it has been recognized that to focus solely upon formal institutional failings and imperfections ignores the role played by informal institutions (Godfrey 2015; North 1990; Scott 2008). As a result, greater attention has been paid to informal institutions, and the informal economy has been increasingly viewed as arising "because of the incongruence between what is defined as legitimate by formal and informal institutions" (Webb *et al.* 2009: 495). This book advances a third way of utilizing institutional theory to explain the informal economy, one that synthesizes these two viewpoints. I argue that formal institutional failings result in an asymmetry between formal and informal institutions, and that this then leads to the greater prevalence of the informal economy.

First-wave institutionalist explanations: formal institutional failures and imperfections

In the first wave of institutionalist thought regarding the informal economy, it was recognized that institutions are "the rules of the game" which prescribe, monitor, enforce and support what is socially acceptable (Baumol & Blinder 2008; Denzau & North 1994; Mathias *et al.* 2014; North 1990; Webb *et al.* 2009) and that there are both codified laws and regulations (i.e., formal institutions) that define the legal rules of the game, as well as informal institutions that convey the norms, values and beliefs of citizens and entrepreneurs about what is acceptable. However, the focus was near enough entirely upon the formal institutions when explaining the prevalence of the informal economy. The view was that the informal economy is a direct result of formal institutional failures and imperfections.

These formal institutional failures that result in larger informal economies are of four types: resource misallocations and inefficiencies; voids and weaknesses; powerlessness; and instability and uncertainty (for an alternative review, see Webb & Ireland 2015). Each is here considered in turn.

Formal institutional resource misallocations and inefficiencies

Resource misallocations and inefficiencies are the result of either the lack of modernization of government organizations and/or government organizations operating in a corrupt way to protect or maximize economic rents for elites. Such resource misallocations and efficiencies are manifested in three ways. First, the public services lack redistributive justice. Citizens do not perceive themselves as receiving the goods or services they deserve given the amount of tax and social contributions they pay (Kinsey & Gramsick 1993; Richardson & Sawyer 2001; Thurman *et al.* 1984). This makes them more likely to operate informally. Secondly, governments lack procedural justice. Citizens will not view the government as treating them in a respectful, impartial and responsible manner (Braithwaite & Reinhart 2000; Murphy 2005). This again results in informality (Hartner *et al.* 2008; Murphy 2003; Murphy *et al.* 2009). Thirdly, public services lack procedural fairness. Citizens will feel they are not treated fairly relative to others (Kinsey & Gramsick 1993), which again leads to informality (Bird *et al.* 2006; McGee *et al.* 2008; Molero & Pujol 2012).

Besides these resource misallocations and inefficiencies resulting from the lack of modernization of state authorities, resource misallocations and inefficiencies also result from the state protecting or maximizing economic rents for elites (Acemoglu & Robinson 2012) and/or the existence of corruption (Aidis & Van Praag 2007; Khan & Quaddus 2015; Round *et al.* 2008; Tonoyan *et al.* 2010). Again, three kinds of corruption exist, each of which has different impacts on the informal economy.

First, and most common, is the "misuse of public office for private gain" (Bardhan 1997; Pope 2000; Shleifer & Vishny 1993; Svensson 2005). This form of corruption occurs when government officials demand or receive gifts, bribes and other payments (e.g. a portion of a given contract) from enterprises and entrepreneurs and provide a service in return. This service might include speeding up the granting of an operating license, not giving a negative outcome from a workplace inspection, or helping enterprises and entrepreneurs avoid delays in processes requiring the approval of public sector officials such as receiving a construction permit. This kind of corruption not only leads to resource misallocations and inefficiencies, but can also arguably force employers, workers and citizens into the informal economy to escape extortion from public officials, which has a negative overall impact on economic development and growth (Williams & Kedir 2016; Williams & Martinez-Perez 2016; Williams *et al.* 2016b).

A second type of corruption, which has been less studied, is state capture. This is where firms or groups of firms influence the formulation of laws and other government policies to their advantage through illicit or non-transparent means (Fries *et al.* 2003). The outcome can be preferential treatment or state resources might be diverted to them. For those not part of these elites, the result is often more burdensome taxes, registration and licensing regulations and costs, which act as a barrier to entry to the formal economy, and fewer public services received for the taxes and social contributions they pay (De Soto 1989; Siqueira *et al.* 2016; Williams *et al.* 2016a).

A third kind of corruption, again seldom studied, is when citizens, workers and employers use personal connections to gain preferential access to public goods and services and/or to circumvent formal procedures. This is variously referred to as *blat* in post-Soviet spaces (Ledeneva 2013; Williams & Onoshchenko 2014, 2015), *guanxi* in China (Chen *et al.* 2012), *wasta* in the Arab world (Smith *et al.* 2011), *jeitinho* in Brazil (Ferreira *et al.* 2012), "pulling strings" in English-speaking countries (Smith *et al.* 2012), *veze* in Serbia, Croatia, and Bosnia and Herzegovina, *vrski* in FYR Macedonia (Williams & Bezeredi 2017), and *vruzki* in Bulgaria (Williams & Yang 2017). This has negative consequences on those playing entirely by the formal rulebook (see Williams & Yang 2017).

Formal institutional voids and weaknesses

Another formal institutional failing and imperfection resulting in greater informality is the existence of formal institutional voids and weaknesses. Indeed, the debates between neoliberal and political economy theory, already discussed, are essentially debates about which institutional voids and weaknesses lead to a greater prevalence of the informal economy. As this view reveals, institutional voids seen as a weakness of economies by some scholars are seen as strengths by others. To explain, a key debate has been whether the informal economy is a result of too little state intervention, as political economy theory argues, or whether participants voluntarily decide to exit the formal sector because of too much state interference, as neoliberal theory argues.

Formal institutional powerlessness

A third formal institutional failing and imperfection resulting in greater informality is formal institutional powerlessness. This powerlessness is expressed in not only a lack of capacity to enforce policies (Webb *et al.* 2009) but also a lack of power to provide incentives to encourage adherence to the formal rules. If we take power to mean the ability to get somebody else to do something that they were not before going to do, in the way in which you want them to do it, formal institutions, especially in the developing world, currently lack power. They possess an inability to make employers, workers and citizens adhere to the formal rules (i.e. the codified laws and regulations).

Two basic tools can be used by formal institutions to achieve adherence to the rules. On the one hand, there are deterrence measures which increase the penalties and risks of detection for those participating in the informal economy (i.e., "sticks"). On the other hand, there are incentives and rewards for compliant behaviour ("carrots"). In many countries, however, formal institutions do not have the capacity and capability to implement effective "sticks" and "carrots" to prevent informal economic activity.

This lack of power of authorities is instantly observable when one recognizes the low costs and high benefits of informal economic activity, and the low benefits and high costs of operating in the formal economy, in many developing countries. The result is that many weigh up the costs and benefits and participate in the informal economy. This is because the benefits of operating formally in developing countries are insufficient to outweigh the benefits of informality (Kistruck *et al.* 2015; Wunsch-Vincent *et al.* 2015). The solution is to enhance the ability of authorities to alter the cost/benefit ratio. Nevertheless, even if the power of authorities is improved to increase the costs of informality and benefits of formality, other formal institutional failings may well remain, as will now be shown.

Formal institutional instability and uncertainty

A fourth and final formal institutional failing relates to the perceived and/or actual instability and uncertainty of the formal rules. Formal institutional instability and uncertainty results from continuous changes in laws and regulations (Levitsky & Murillo 2009; Williams & Shahid 2016). In many developing and transition economies, citizens, workers and employers witness continuous changes in the formal rules, meaning that they do not expect rules that apply today to remain the same in the future. In many transition economies, for example, citizens, workers and employers do not see the rationale in making compulsory contributory payments for pensions, or social contributions so they can claim unemployment benefits, because they believe that in the future they will not benefit because different rules will apply. This perceived lack of permanency of the formal rules is a key problem that leads many to evade payments. Put another way, the power of authorities to implement formalization is constrained by the lack of trust in authorities in the medium to long term.

In many developing and transition economies, furthermore, there is often a view that the formal rules that exist are not indigenous to the country and/

or are imposed by external supranational institutions. This was particularly prominent during the early stages of transformation in the post-socialist countries of East-Central Europe (see Williams *et al.* 2013). It is also prevalent in the developing world, not least when the IMF impose specific structural adjustment conditions onto countries, and the population do not therefore see the formal rules as decided by, or belonging to, the national government but as imposed by outside forces. In these contexts, particularly when the laws and regulations (i.e. "state morale") are continuously changing, citizens, workers and employers turn elsewhere for a more permanent set of values, norms and understandings, namely informal institutions, in relation to what is acceptable and what is not. This is often because these informal rules of the game are more enduring and turned to when formal institutions continuously change the rules. Indeed, developing economies are perhaps so defined precisely because they have underdeveloped formal institutions which can be very fluid and temporary in nature, and result in citizens, workers and employers turning to socially shared norms, values and beliefs to facilitate, govern and structure their economic activities instead of formal rules (London *et al.* 2014; Mair *et al.* 2012).

Second-wave institutional thought: informal institutions and institutional asymmetry

A second wave of institutional theory pays more attention than the first to the prominent role played by informal institutions. It argues that the informal economy does not result from formal institutional failings and imperfections, but rather, only does so if the socially shared norms, values and beliefs are not aligned with the formal rules (Godfrey 2015; Webb *et al.* 2009; Williams & Horodnic 2015a, 2015b).

From this neo-institutionalist theoretical perspective, the behaviour of citizens, workers and employers is shaped by their institutional environments. According to Richard Scott (2008), such institutional environments comprise three pillars, namely the regulative, normative and cultural-cognitive. The regulatory pillar is composed of the formal rules, laws and associated sanctions that encourage some behaviours and restrict others, such as the formal rules about paying taxes, declaring work, and the terms and conditions of employment. The normative pillar is composed of the norms, beliefs and values regarding acceptable behaviour (i.e., the social acceptability of working informally, or purchasing goods and services from the informal economy). The cultural-cognitive pillar relates to how certain taken-for-granted behaviours emerge grounded in shared understandings, such as how routine purchasing from an informal vendor, or not expecting or asking for receipts, is enacted unthinkingly. This cultural-cognitive pillar is most clearly displayed when informal practices are referred to as "cultural" or culturally embedded, such as when the populations of countries state that informality is part of, for example, the Balkan mentality, the Greek way, Slavic culture, the African mind-set, and so on.

This second wave of institutionalist theory asserts that the behaviour of employers, citizens and workers reflects these regulatory, normative and cognitive rules in their institutional environments, and gives them legitimacy. Legitimacy in the regulative pillar means compliance with the formal rules; in the normative pillar it is based on conformity with a moral basis; and in the cultural-cognitive pillar it is based on adopting a common frame of meaning (Scott 2008). Institutions thus exert pressure for compliance through various mechanisms of isomorphism.

Coercive isomorphism is largely associated with the formal regulatory institutional pillar and the enforcement of formal rules and laws. This either enforces compliance using "sticks" or rewards and encourages compliant behaviour using "carrots". Normative isomorphism, meanwhile, is associated with pressures to conform to wider societal expectations, and mimetic isomorphism is related to the cultural-cognitive pillar, whereby citizens, workers and employers act in ways reflecting shared understandings which are culturally supported. The latter two are here conflated under the umbrella of informal institutions, which is the norm in studies explaining the prevalence of the informal economy from this second-wave perspective.

This second-wave theory, on the one hand, examines the asymmetry between informal and formal institutions, and on the other hand, develops a theory of informal adjustments, which refers to citizens, workers and employers using the norms, values and beliefs in their society to facilitate, govern and structure their economic activities rather than the formal laws, regulations and supporting apparatuses (Webb & Ireland 2015). Importantly, these norms, values and beliefs are the basis for collective shared rules, whether implicitly held or formally codified. Indeed, London *et al.* (2014) reveal how the influence of informal institutions becomes greater when there are formal institutional failures and imperfections.

Hence, in second-wave thought, formal institutional failings per se do not result in the greater prevalence of the informal economy. If formal and informal institutions align and are complementary, then the informal economy will not result from formal institutional failings. This is because citizens, workers and employers will adhere to the formal rules. The informal economy will only occur unintentionally, such as due to the rules being too complex to fulfil.

Formal institutional failings and imperfections only result in a growth in the informal economy when there is asymmetry between the formal and informal institutions, and thus the rules of informal institutions are incompatible with, and substitute for, those of the formal institutions (see Godfrey 2011, 2015; Webb *et al.* 2009; Williams & Shahid 2016; Williams *et al.* 2015; Windebank & Horodnic 2017). This is often termed "institutional asymmetry" (Williams *et al.* 2016a). The informal economy arises "because of the incongruence between what is defined as legitimate by formal and informal institutions" (Webb *et al.* 2009: 495). It is therefore only when formal and informal institutions do not align, as is commonly the case in many developing countries, that the informal economy prevails, which although formally illegal, is deemed socially legitimate (De Castro *et al.* 2014; Kistruck *et al.* 2015; Siqueira *et al.* 2016; Webb *et al.* 2013, 2014). Indeed, the greater the non-alignment between formal and informal institutions, the greater is the prevalence of the informal economy (Williams & Shahid 2016). Informal economic activity is consequently endeavour that occurs outside of the formal rules but within the norms, values and beliefs of informal institutions (Godfrey 2011; Kistruck *et al.* 2015; Siqueira *et al.* 2016; Webb *et al.* 2009; Welter *et al.* 2015).

In order to evaluate and measure whether informal economic practices are deemed socially legitimate by informal institutions, studies have been conducted on citizens' attitudes towards paying taxes, referred to in the literature as "tax morale". These have found that the prevalence of the informal economy and level of tax morale are strongly correlated, with Pearson r values[1] between -0.51 and -0.66 (Alm & Torgler 2006; Alm *et al.* 2006; Barone & Mocetti 2009; Frey 1997; Halla 2010; Lewis 1982; Pommerehne

---

1. Pearson's r or the Pearson correlation coefficient is a measure of the linear correlation between two variables. Its value is between +1 and −1, where 1 is total positive linear correlation, 0 is no linear correlation, and −1 is total negative linear correlation.

& Weck-Hanneman 1996; Riahi-Belkaoui 2004; Richardson 2006; Torgler 2005, 2011; Torgler & Schneider 2009). The higher the level of tax morale (i.e., citizens' willingness to pay taxes), the smaller is the informal economy. Examining Europe and the United States, James Alm and Benno Torgler (2006) find a strong negative correlation (Pearson r = -0.460) significant at the 0.05 level, and that tax morale explains more than 20 per cent of the total variance in the size of the informal economy. If tax morale declines (i.e., citizens become less willing to pay taxes), therefore, the informal economy will increase. In transition economies, meanwhile, Alm *et al.* (2006) again find a strong negative correlation (-0.657), and that tax morale explains over 30 per cent of the total variance in the size of the informal economy.

Third-wave institutionalist thought: institutional asymmetry as an outcome of formal institutional failures

In first-wave thought, formal institutional failings and imperfections were seen to result in the prevalence of the informal economy. In second-wave thought, however, it was recognized that even if there are formal institutional failings, the informal economy only results when the socially shared norms, values and beliefs are not aligned with the formal rules.

In third-wave thought, however, the argument is that the informal economy is not solely produced by institutional asymmetry per se. Such institutional asymmetry is itself a result of formal institutional failings and imperfections. It is argued that formal institutional failings and imperfections produce an asymmetry between formal and informal institutions, and this then leads to the greater prevalence of the informal economy (Williams 2018). In order to advance this third-wave thought, we first need to understand the precise formal institutional imperfections that lead to institutional asymmetry and thus larger informal economies, and then we can examine how these formal institutional failings and imperfections can best be tackled. These are the two key objectives addressed in the rest of this book. To start to do so, the next chapter turns to evaluating the structural or country-level conditions (i.e. formal institutional failings and imperfections) that influence the size of the informal economy.

3

Measuring the size of the informal economy

Introduction

Those hearing figures regarding the size of the informal economy for the first time, akin to more seasoned scholars, are correct to be deeply sceptical about these estimates of its magnitude. Not only is the informal economy by its very nature a hidden phenomenon and therefore difficult to measure but estimates of its size often vary markedly. For example, estimates of the size of the informal economy in Romania range from 9.5 to 37.8 per cent of GDP, and in Germany from 1.0 to 17.1 per cent (GHK & Fondazione Brodolini 2009). To understand such startlingly different measurements of the size of the informal economy, however, it is necessary to comprehend the various methods being used to measure its magnitude.

In this chapter, therefore, the next section briefly introduces the various measurement methods. These range from indirect methods that seek statistical traces of the informal economy in data collected for other purposes to more direct survey methods. Following this, the third section then reports a study of the variations in the size of the informal economy in the European Union using an indirect measurement method, namely the labour input method (LIM), and then uses these estimates to evaluate the theories discussed in the last chapter by comparing whether there is a significant correlation between cross-national variations in the size of the informal economy using this indirect measurement method and cross-national variations in the structural determinants highlighted to be important in each theorization. This is then followed, in the fourth section, by a reporting of the cross-national variations in the size of the informal economy in developing countries using a direct survey approach, along with whether similar correlations are identified between the size of the informal economy and various structural determinants. The fifth and final section then draws some conclusions about the measurement methods and the validity of the different theorizations discussed in the last chapter that seek to explain the country-level variations in the size of the informal economy.

Methods for measuring the size of the informal economy

Two broad types of method exist for measuring the size of the informal economy: indirect and direct. For those who assume that respondents will not report whether they participate in the informal economy, indirect methods are preferred. These use macroeconomic data collected and/or constructed for other purposes. The belief is that even if those participating in the informal economy hide their activity, statistical traces of its existence will be revealed in macroeconomic data collected for other purposes. On the other hand, there are those who assert that although informal economy activity might be illegal in terms of the laws and regulations of formal institutions, it is often deemed a legitimate endeavour in the eyes of the informal institutions (i.e. the norms, values and beliefs of workers, citizens and employers). As such, and unlike criminal activity which is both illegal and illegitimate activity, activity in the informal economy is more hidden in plain sight and usually openly discussed by participants, which makes data collection feasible using direct survey methods. Each method is here examined in turn.

Indirect measurement methods

Indirect methods seek evidence of the size of the informal economy in macroeconomic data collected and/or constructed for other purposes. The indirect methods can be grouped into four types according to the indicators used to measure the size of the informal economy: non-monetary indicator methods; monetary proxy indicator methods; income/expenditure discrepancy methods; and multiple indicator methods.

Non-monetary indicator methods
The most common non-monetary indicator methods are first, those using very small enterprises as a proxy, secondly, those using electricity demand as a surrogate, and thirdly, those seeking traces in formal labour force statistics.

The first non-monetary method uses very small enterprises (VSEs) as a proxy indicator of the size of the informal economy (e.g. ILO 2002a, 2002b; Portes & Sassen-Koob 1987; US General Accounting Office 1989). As a proxy indicator of the magnitude of the informal economy however, this VSE approach is subject to two contradictory assumptions. On the one hand, not all VSEs are in the informal economy, which could lead to an overestimate. On the other hand, fully unregistered VSEs will escape government record keeping and could lead to an underestimate (Portes 1994). It also ignores individual types of informal work undertaken on a one-to-one basis, which recent surveys reveal constitutes a large proportion of the informal economy in developed countries (European Commission 2014b).

A second non-monetary method uses electricity demand as a surrogate indicator of the size of the informal economy (e.g. Friedman *et al* 2000; Lacko 1999). Economic activity and electricity consumption are asserted to move in step with each other with an electricity-to-GDP elasticity of close to one, meaning that the growth of total electricity consumption is a reliable indicator for the growth of overall (formal and informal) GDP. By using this measure and subtracting the official GDP, the size of the informal economy is estimated. The problems with this method are threefold: (1) many types of informal work do not require a considerable amount of electricity (e.g. personal services); (2) other energy sources can be used (e.g. gas, oil, coal); (3) using this to measure temporal changes does not account for increases in energy efficiency or how alterations in the elasticity of electricity-to-GDP vary across countries and over time (Andrews *et al.* 2011).

A third non-monetary method seeks traces of the informal economy in formal labour force statistics. One method using formal labour force statistics measures unaccountable increases in the number employed in various types of employment (e.g. self-employment, second-job holding) as a proxy indicator of the size of the informal economy (e.g. Crnkovic-Pozaic 1999; Del Boca & Forte 1982; Hellberger & Schwarze 1986). However, the idea that the informal economy prevails in these categories of employment is an assumption, rather than an evidence-based finding, and it is difficult to know whether the increase is due to informal work, rather than other factors. Another measurement method using labour force statistics examines discrepancies in the results of different official surveys, such as the population census and firm surveys (e.g. Flaming *et al.* 2005; Lobo 1990; Mattera 1985; US Congress Joint Economic Committee 1983). Again, whether the variations identified are purely due to the informal economy, or whether other survey design issues or factors are involved, is difficult to discern. A further and popular application of the use of labour force statistics is the discrepancy method that compares the findings of surveys of the supply of labour, such as labour force surveys (LFS), with surveys of the recorded labour demand (e.g. based on company declarations to tax or social security authorities or national statistical offices). Sometimes known as the labour input method (LIM), a study using this to estimate the size of the informal economy in the European Union will be detailed below.

Monetary indicator methods

Besides using non-monetary surrogate indicators, other studies use monetary proxies. Three principal monetary proxies have been used, namely large denomination notes, the cash-deposit ratio, and money transactions.

Measurement methods using large denomination notes as a proxy indicator of the size of the informal economy assume that those working in the informal economy use exclusively cash in their transactions and that large sums are involved with high denomination notes exchanged (Bartlett 1998; Henry 1976; Matthews 1982). However, this approach is problematic. First, it cannot separate the use of large denomination notes used in criminal activities from those used for transactions in the informal economy (Bartlett 1998). Secondly, many informal economy transactions are for small amounts of money (Cornuel & Duriez 1985; European Commission 2014b) and thirdly, many other factors besides the informal economy, such as changes in the modes of payment (e.g. credit cards, store cards) influence the use of large denomination bank notes.

A second monetary proxy of the size of the informal economy is the ratio of currency in circulation to demand deposits. This is known as the cash-deposit ratio approach. Based on the assumption that informal economy transactions occur in cash, this estimates the currency in circulation required by formal economy activities and subtracts this from the actual money in circulation. The difference, multiplied by the velocity of money, is the currency in circulation due to the informal economy. The ratio of this figure to the observed GDP measures the informal economy as a proportion of the total economy. Pioneered by Gutmann (1977) in the United States, this method has been widely adopted (Caridi & Passerini 2001; Cocco & Santos 1984; Matthews 1983; Matthews & Rastogi 1985; Tanzi 1980). However, it too suffers from major problems. First, cash is not always the medium of exchange for informal economy transactions (e.g. Contini 1982; Smith 1985). Secondly, it cannot distinguish the share of cash in circulation that is due to the informal economy and the proportion that is due to crime, nor how this is changing over time. Thirdly, the choice of the cash-deposit ratio as a proxy is arbitrary and not derived from economic theory (e.g. Trundle 1982). Fourthly, the cash-deposit ratio is influenced by many other factors besides solely the informal economy (e.g. changing methods of payment, financial exclusion), often working in opposite directions to one another. Fifthly, the choice of a base period when the informal economy supposedly did not exist is problematic, especially given the sensitivity of the results to which base year is chosen (Thomas 1986). Sixthly, it assumes the same velocity of cash circulation in the informal and formal economies when there is no evidence (Frey & Weck 1983), and finally, it is impossible to determine how much of the currency of a country is held domestically and how much abroad (Feige 2012).

Recognizing that electronic payments and cheques are used in informal economy transactions as well as cash, a third monetary approach estimates the extent to which the total quantity of monetary transactions exceed what would be predicted in the absence of the informal economy (Feige 1979, 2012). As evidence that cheques and electronic payments as well as cash are used in the informal economy in the United States, Edgar Feige (1990) quotes a study by the Internal Revenue Service (IRS) showing that between a quarter and third of unreported income was paid by cheque rather than currency. In Norway, similarly, Isachsen *et al.* (1982) find that in 1980, 20 per cent of informal services were paid for with a cheque, whilst a study of Detroit (Smith 1985) provides an even higher estimate, in the realm of informal economy home repair, finding that bills were settled roughly equally in cheques and cash. This approach however, suffers the same problems as the cash-deposit approach. The only problem it overcomes is the acceptance that informal economy transactions involve electronic payments and cheques. Hence, the above criticisms are not here repeated.

Income/expenditure discrepancies

This approach evaluates differences in expenditure and income at either the aggregate national or household level. It is grounded in the belief that participants in the informal economy might hide their incomes but cannot hide their expenditures. An assessment of income/expenditure discrepancies is therefore believed to be capable of revealing the magnitude of the informal economy.

Aggregate-level studies analyse the discrepancy between national expenditure and income to estimate the size of the informal economy. Such studies have been conducted in Canada (Morissette 2014), Germany (e.g. Langfelt 1989), Sweden (e.g. Apel 1994), the UK (e.g. O'Higgins 1989) and the United States (e.g. Macafee 1980; Paglin 1994). Studies of income/expenditure discrepancies at the household level, meanwhile, use household income and expenditure data to estimate the size of the informal economy via income under-reporting (Dilnot & Morris 1981; Macafee 1980; O'Higgins 1989). For the discrepancy between income and expenditure to be a measure of the size of the informal economy, assumptions must be made about the accuracy of the income and expenditure data.

On the expenditure side, estimates depend upon the accurate declaration of expenditure. Philip Mattera (1985) suggests that most people cannot estimate their spending because few people keep expenditure records, unlike income, which for employees arrives in regular recorded uniform tranches. On the income side meanwhile, it is difficult to know whether this derives from criminal or informal work, or even from savings. In addition, problems exist of non-response and under-reporting (Thomas 1992). Hence, the accuracy of this method is doubtful. Hannelore Weck-Hannemann and Bruno Frey (1985) clearly display this when they show that the national income in Switzerland is larger than expenditure, suggesting that the Swiss informal economy must be negative, which is nonsensical and reveals that this discrepancy is not an indicator of the size of the informal economy.

Multiple indicator methods

The indirect measurement methods so far discussed use single proxy indicators of the size of the informal economy. Multiple indicator approaches, the most popular of which is the DYMIMIC (dynamic multiple indicators multiple causes) approach, consider multiple indicators and multiple causes (e.g. Schneider & Williams 2013; Williams & Schneider 2016). In this method, the informal economy is an unobserved (or latent) variable that influences observed indicators and is determined by observed variables. Schneider (2001) views the causes of the informal economy as the burden of direct and indirect taxation (both actual and perceived), the burden of regulation and tax morale (citizens' attitudes towards paying taxes). First, therefore, this method examines the determinants (e.g. real and perceived tax burden, the burden of regulation, tax morale) and indicators (male participation rate, hours worked and growth of real GDP) and secondly, calculates the size of the informal economy with the aid of econometric tools.

However, all these supposed causes and the indicators used are questionable. For example, numerous studies reveal that cross-national variations in taxation rates, whatever measure of taxation is used, are either not correlated with the informal economy or the association is not in the direction assumed in this model (Eurofound 2013; Vanderseypen *et al.* 2013; Williams 2013a, 2013b, 2013c). Similarly, many studies reveal that one cannot assume that the burden of regulation per se results in an increase in the size of the informal economy; it depends on the type of regulation considered (Williams & Renooy 2014). Care is thus required when using this measurement method. Nevertheless, it has grown in popularity (e.g. Bajada & Schneider 2005; Chatterjee *et al.* 2002; Giles 1999a, 1999b; Giles & Tedds 2002). Indirect measurement methods however, are not the only techniques used to estimate the size of the informal economy.

Direct measurement methods

Rather than use indirect indicator methods to evaluate the size of the informal economy, direct surveys can be employed. Those advocating direct methods criticize the indirect methods for being unreliable and inaccurate, and using crude assumptions concerning its nature that are far from proven (Thomas 1992; Williams 2004c; Williams & Windebank 1998, 1999). In previous decades when little empirical survey data was available, such indirect indicator methods undoubtedly played an important role in highlighting the existence of the informal economy. Today, however, the growing number of direct surveys means that indirect methods are no longer as necessary as was previously the case (Williams 2006a).

The major criticism of direct survey methods from proponents of indirect methods is that they naively assume that people will reveal to them, or even know, about their participation in the informal economy. On the one hand, purchasers may not even know if the goods and services purchased are from the informal economy and on the other hand, sellers will be reticent about disclosing the extent of their informal work. The former point might well be valid. However, it is not necessarily the case that those supplying work in the informal economy will be untruthful in their dealings with researchers. As Liliana Bàculo (2001: 2) states regarding her face-to-face interviews, "they were curious and flattered that university researchers were interested in their problems" and were more than willing to share their experiences. Ray Pahl (1984) similarly found that when comparing the results from individuals as suppliers and purchasers, the same level of informal work was discovered. The implication therefore is that individuals are not secretive about the informal work they supply.

Similar conclusions are reached about the openness of research participants in Canada (Fortin *et al.* 1996) and the UK (Leonard 1994; MacDonald 1994; Williams 2004c). As Robert MacDonald (1994) reveals in his study of the unemployed in a deprived region of the UK, "fiddly work" was not a sensitive subject to participants. They happily talked about it in the same breath as discussing for instance their experiences of starting up in self-employment or of voluntary work. This willingness to talk openly about informal work was also found in Belfast (Leonard 1994). Indeed, neither are there grounds for assuming that businesses will not report their participation in the informal economy. In one of the few direct surveys that interviews businesses about the extent of their participation in the informal economy, the 2002 EBRD/World Bank Business Environment and Enterprise Performance Survey conducted in 26 countries of East-Central Europe and the Commonwealth of Independent States (CIS), Fries *et al.* (2003) find that it is wholly possible to collect such data. There have also been several qualitative surveys that again reveal the willingness of both employers and employees to openly talk about their participation in the informal economy (e.g. Jones *et al.* 2004; Ram *et al.* 2001, 2002a, 2002b, 2003, 2007). This is perhaps because although informal work is illegal in terms of the laws and regulations of formal institutions, it is deemed legitimate endeavour from the perspective of informal institutions, namely the norms, values and beliefs of the population (Webb *et al.* 2009). Consequently, it is openly discussed which makes reliable collection possible using direct survey methods.

Here, therefore, are the results regarding the size of the informal economy of a recent cross-national comparative survey using an indirect approach, followed by a study using the direct survey method.

The indirect approach: estimating the informal economy in the European Union using the labour input method

The labour input method (LIM) is an indirect non-monetary indicator method. It estimates the size of the informal economy by measuring the difference/discrepancy between the reported labour supply by workers (as reported in the European Union Labour Force Surveys) and the reported use of labour by employers (as reported in enterprise and business surveys) after generating a harmonized database to make the two key data sources comparable.

In what follows the first step is to provide a description of how LIM generates estimates of the size of the informal economy, along with the data sources and variables used. Secondly, the results are reported on the variable size of the informal economy and in the final step, the correlations are analysed between the estimates of its variable size and various structural determinants to evaluate the competing theories discussed in the last chapter.

1. The method: LIM

The labour input method (LIM) is an indirect measurement method that measures the size of the informal economy using macroeconomic data to identify the discrepancy between the reported supply of labour inputs (from the Labour Force Survey) and demand-side data on recorded labour demand (e.g. from enterprise surveys, company declarations to tax or social security authorities, or national statistical offices). The discrepancy between the two provides an estimate of magnitude of the informal economy. The underlying premise is that firms may deliberately conceal part of their economic activities and therefore part of their labour input into the production of goods and services, and that by identifying the discrepancies in the labour inputs reported by businesses in enterprise surveys, and the labour inputs reported by individuals in labour force surveys, an estimate of the scale of the informal economy can be produced.

LIM, therefore, is based on the following steps (OECD 2002):

1. Estimate the labour input underlying GDP estimates from the demand-side using enterprise surveys;

2. Estimate the labour input from the supply-side based on household survey data which are obtained from a labour force survey (LFS) supplemented by population registers or census data if these are available;

3. Standardize the labour input estimates by converting both sources to the same units of labour input, such as hours worked or full-time equivalent employment units;

4. Compare the two sets of estimates and assess potential discrepancies taking account of the reliability of the different sources.

The OECD (2002) define a set of procedures which should be followed when converting the discrepancies in labour inputs into an estimate of this as a percentage of gross value added (GVA). It states that analysts should:

1. Obtain estimates of the labour supply disaggregated on the level of economic activity and size of enterprise or type of labour (employees, self-employed), from a labour force survey and/or other supplementary demographic sources;

2. Obtain estimates of output per unit of labour input and value added per unit of labour input for the same activity and size breakdown from regular statistical enterprise surveys; and

3. Multiply the labour input estimates from (1) by ratios expressed in the per unit terms which results in output and value added for the activity and size categories.

The labour inputs estimated in step 1 are used as weights that should be applied to the enterprise survey output estimates and value added per unit of labour input (derived in step 2). To calculate the informal economy component of the GVA, ratios of output and value added per unit of labour input are used, which are taken from enterprise surveys (SBS).

Below, the discrepancy in labour inputs reported from the supply- and demand-side are reported for each EU member state (for a detailed analysis, see Williams *et al.* 2018). To do this, the demand-side labour inputs are calculated using the national accounts (NAs) while the supply-side is examined using the European Union Labour Force Survey (EU LFS). Given that the structural business statistics (SBS) cover only the private sector, the estimate of the size of the informal economy is confined to an analysis of the proportion of labour inputs that is in the informal economy in the private sector.

2. The results: the variable size of the informal economy

Figures 3.1 and 3.2 present the estimates of the proportion of the private sector that is in the informal economy in the EU. On average across EU member states, 11.6 per cent of total labour input in the private sector is in the informal economy, and the informal economy constitutes on average 16.4 per cent of GVA in the private sector, this higher figure being because informal labour is concentrated in sectors where labour productivity is higher.

These, however, are unweighted averages, and do not take account of the relative size of the labour force in each country (Eurostat 2017). The weighted averages are that 9.3 per cent of total labour input in the private sector is in the informal economy, and the informal economy constitutes 14.3 per cent of GVA in the private sector. The reason for the weighted average being lower than the unweighted average is due to the influence of larger countries such as Germany, France and the UK, which have larger labour forces and relatively lower levels of informal work.

The informal economy, however, is not everywhere of the same magnitude. As Figure 3.1 reveals, the countries with informal economies larger than the EU average are largely new EU member states (NMS). Among the

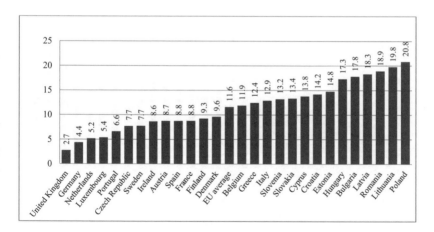

Figure 3.1 Informal work in the private sector in the EU, 2013 (% of total labour input)

Note: estimates for Malta are not provided due to the inadequacy of the data for this member state.

Source: derived from Williams *et al.* (2018)

older members only Italy is included. On the other hand, only the Czech Republic from the NMS has a smaller than EU average informal economy. The lowest share of informal work in terms of labour input is recorded for the UK, Germany and the Netherlands where less than 3 per cent of the total labour input is in the informal economy.

As Figure 3.2 reveals, the distribution of countries does not change significantly when the informal economy is measured as a proportion of GVA in the private sector. The informal economy is highest in Poland, Romania and Lithuania where it is greater than 25 per cent of total GVA created in the private sector. Those countries with informal economies larger than the EU average are again mostly new member states (Hungary, Latvia, Estonia, Bulgaria, Cyprus, Croatia and Czech Republic) along with only three older EU members: Greece, Spain and Italy. Only Slovakia and Slovenia from the group of NMS countries have informal economies slightly below the EU average. It is to be noted that even in the economy with the lowest share of informal work, namely Germany, it is still 7 per cent of private sector GVA.

Not only the size of the informal economy but also the structure of the informal labour market differs across EU member states. As Figure 3.3 reveals, in the EU, 61.8 per cent of all informal work is conducted by

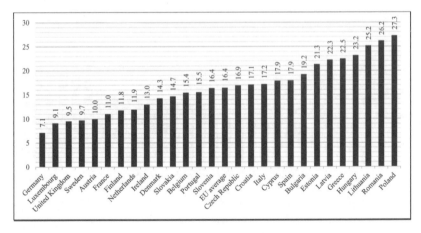

Figure 3.2 Informal work in the private sector, 2013 (% of total GVA)

Note: estimates for Malta are not provided due to deficiencies of data sources for this member state

Source: derived from Williams *et al.* (2018)

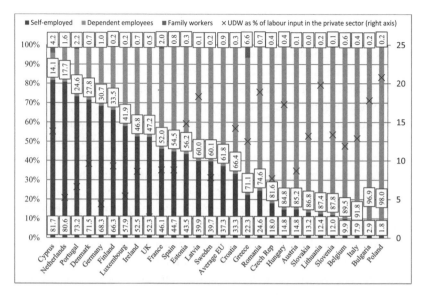

Figure 3.3 Informal economy in EU countries, 2013 (by type of employment)

Source: derived from Williams *et al.* (2018)

employees, 37.3 per cent by the self-employed and 0.3 per cent by family workers (i.e. persons working in a family business or on a family farm without pay and who are living in the same household as the owner of the business or farm and receive remuneration in the form of fringe benefits or payments in kind). However, this markedly varies across countries.

In some countries, the informal economy is largely composed of the self-employed (e.g. Cyprus, Netherlands and Portugal) but this is not the case in others. In a significant number of countries, such as Bulgaria and Poland, it is much more of an issue related to waged employees who are employed on either a wholly informal (i.e. unregistered) basis or who are engaged in quasi-formal employment (i.e. with a portion of their salary being paid as an informal envelope wage). Comparing Poland and Denmark for example, in Poland, 25.3 per cent of dependent employment is undertaken in the informal economy (measured in terms of total labour inputs), but only 2.5 per cent of self-employment is in the informal economy, and 5.7 per cent of the labour inputs of family workers are undeclared. The result is that 98 per cent of all informal work is conducted by employees. In Denmark, in stark contrast, only 3 per cent of dependent employment is conducted in the informal economy, but 58.9 per cent of self-employment and 58.9 per cent of family work. The result is that 71.5 per cent of all informal work is conducted by the self-employed.

These differences in the structure of the informal labour market across the EU have significant implications for tackling the informal economy. Policy initiatives to help businesses start-up on a legitimate basis, such as smoothing the transition from unemployment to self-employment, will therefore be useful in tackling the informal economy in Denmark (and other countries where most informal work is conducted by the self-employed) and less relevant to tackling the informal economy in Poland and other countries where most informal work is conducted by employees. Meanwhile, policy initiatives to address unregistered or underdeclared waged employment, such as the use of notification letters to employers and employees to change behaviour, will be relevant to tackling the informal economy in Poland and other countries where most informal work is conducted by employees, but much less relevant in Denmark and other countries where most informal work is conducted by the self-employed. It is not only the development of tailored policy measures, however, that member states need to pursue to tackle the informal economy.

3. Analysis: explaining the variable size of the informal economy in the European Union

Using this data, an analysis can be undertaken of the relationship between cross-national variations in the level of participation in the informal economy and the economic and social characteristics that each theorization outlined in Chapter 2 views as determinants. Given the small sample size of 28 countries and lack of necessary controls to include in a multivariate regression analysis, it is only possible here to conduct bivariate regression analyses. To do this, Spearman's rank correlation coefficient (r_s) is used due to the non-parametric nature of the data.[2] Despite the limitation of only

2. The Spearman correlation between two variables is equal to the Pearson r correlation between the rank values of those two variables (see footnote 1). While Pearson's correlation assesses linear relationships, Spearman's correlation assesses monotonic relationships (whether linear or not). If there are no repeated data values, a perfect Spearman correlation of +1 or −1 occurs when each of the variables is a perfect

using bivariate regression analysis, some meaningful findings are produced regarding the validity of the different theoretical explanations.

Previous studies, using direct survey data, have revealed that the informal economy is higher in member states with: lower levels of GDP per capita; less modern institutions of governance, displayed by higher levels of public sector corruption and lower qualities of governance; low trust in authorities; lower expenditure as a percentage of GDP on active labour market policies; lower levels of social expenditure; less effective social transfer systems; higher levels of severe material deprivation, and higher levels of inequality (Vanderseypen *et al.* 2013; Williams 2014a, 2014b, 2014c, 2015a, 2015b; Williams & Horodnic 2015a, 2016a, 2017; Williams & Kedir 2018a, 2018b, 2018c; Williams & Krasniqi 2018; Williams *et al.* 2015). We can, therefore, test whether this is similarly the case when using the above results of the indirect labour input method.

Evaluating modernization theory in terms of whether cross-national variations in the size of the informal economy (using the LIM estimate of the scale of the informal economy as a percentage of total labour inputs in the private sector) are associated with cross-national variations in the structural conditions viewed as determinants by this theory, the finding is that there is a strong significant relationship between cross-national variations in the size of the informal economy and cross-national variations in both GDP per capita in purchasing power standards ($r_s = -.783^{***}$) as well as the European Quality of Government Index ($r_s = -.686^{***}$). There is also a moderate significant relationship between cross-national variations in the size of the informal economy (using the LIM estimates) and the Corruption Perceptions Index ($r_s = -.597^{***}$). The higher the level of GDP per capita in purchasing power standards, the greater the quality of government and the lower the perceived level of corruption, then the smaller the size of the informal economy. This evidence, therefore, supports the modernization theory of the informal economy that its size is related to the level of economic development and degree of modernization of governance.

---

monotone function of the other. The Spearman correlation between two variables will be high when observations have a similar (or identical for a correlation of 1) rank (i.e. relative position label of the observations within the variable: first, second, third, etc.) between the two variables, and low when observations have a dissimilar (or fully opposed for a correlation of −1) rank between the two variables.

Turning to whether support is also found for the neoliberal theory that the informal economy is a result of high tax rates and state interference or conversely, political economy theory which asserts that it is due to a lack of state intervention in work and welfare, the finding is that the higher is the level of public expenditure on labour market interventions to protect vulnerable groups, the smaller is the informal economy ($r_s = -.507^{***}$) and the greater is the impact of social transfers in reducing poverty, the smaller is the informal economy ($r_s = -.570^{***}$). There is, moreover, no statistically significant relationship between cross-national variations in the implicit tax rate (ITR) on labour and the size of the informal economy ($r_s = -.142$). These findings thus support the political economy explanation for the size of the informal economy and refute the neoliberal explanation.

Finally, and evaluating institutional theory, there is also a strong statistically significant relationship between cross-national variations in the size of the informal economy and cross-national variations in the level of trust in authorities. The finding is that the higher is the level of trust in authorities, the smaller is the size of the informal economy ($r_s = -.597^{***}$).

The direct approach: estimating the size of the informal economy in developing countries

To evaluate the variations in the size of the informal economy in the developing world, along with the determinants of the magnitude of the informal economy, we shall use the International Labour Organization (ILO) estimates of the level of what it terms "employment in the informal economy" across 36 countries.

As with the indirect approach above, we shall first outline the methodology used to estimate the cross-national variations in the size of the informal economy, before presenting the results, and then evaluating the competing explanations for the cross-national variations in the prevalence of the informal economy using this ILO dataset of 36 countries. Before commencing, however, it is important to state that the data here examines what in Chapter 1 was referred to as "employment in the informal economy" (Hussmans 2005; ILO 2011, 2012).

1. Methodology

To measure the level of participation in the informal economy in different countries and evaluate the contrasting explanations for the cross-national variations, we can analyse the ILO surveys conducted in 47 developing countries. In total, data is available for 36 of these 47 countries on the level of employment in the informal economy. This uses a common broad definition across all countries and a similar harmonized survey methodology to collect data using either an ILO Department of Statistics questionnaire sent to countries or information from national labour force or informal economy surveys (for further details, see ILO 2012).

This survey examines only whether the main employment of a person is in the informal economy. It does not include those who have secondary jobs in the informal economy. It also excludes employment in agriculture, hunting, forestry and fishing. If these sectors were included, along with those who have second jobs in the informal economy, the size of the informal economy would be greater. It is often stated that direct surveys underestimate the scale of the informal economy relative to indirect measurement methods (Williams *et al.* 2018). If anything, therefore, participation in the informal economy might be higher than suggested by this survey. As such, some caution is required with this data set. It is likely to provide a lower-bound estimate of the level of participation in the informal economy.

To analyse the relationship between cross-national variations in the level of participation in the informal economy and the economic and social characteristics that each theorization views as determinants, as well as the small sample size of 36 countries and lack of necessary controls to include in a multivariate regression analysis, it is again only possible here to conduct bivariate regression analyses. Spearman's rank correlation coefficient (r_s) is again used due to the non-parametric nature of the data.

2. The results: the size of the informal economy across developing countries

Table 3.1 reports the findings on the level of employment in the informal economy. This reveals that the simple unweighted average is that the majority (57.4%) of the non-agricultural workforce in these 36 countries have

Table 3.1 Employment in the informal economy as percentage of non-agricultural employment (by global region)

Global region	Total employment in the informal economy as % of non-agricultural employment, weighted	Total employment in the informal economy as % of non-agricultural employment, unweighted	Number of countries
Europe and Central Asia	24.8	22.8	4
East Asia & Pacific	47.4	64.8	4
Latin America & Caribbean	51.1	58.2	16
Sub-Saharan Africa	53.1	64.8	8
Middle East & North Africa	58.5	59.0	1
South Asia	75.6	75.9	3
All global regions	59.8	57.4	36

Source: derived from ILO (2012)

their main employment in the informal economy. However, a weighted average figure is here used which accounts for the variable workforce size in each country. Across all 36 countries, three out of every five (59.8%) non-agricultural workers have their main employment in the informal economy. The informal economy, therefore, is not some minor residue of little importance. It is a realm that employs most of the workforce across these developing economies.

However, this overall weighted average figure masks some major variations across global regions. To analyse this, the 36 countries for which data are available are divided, using the World Bank (2013) classification, into six regions. The finding is that the weighted proportion of the non-agricultural workforce whose main job is in the informal economy ranges from one-quarter (24.8%) of the working population in Europe and Central Asia, through to 75.6 per cent in South Asia. As such, the proportion of the working population with their main job in the informal economy is unevenly distributed globally.

As Table 3.2 reports, there are also marked cross-national variations in the proportion of the workforce with their main job in the informal economy, ranging from 84.7 per cent of the non-agricultural workforce in Mali to 6.5 per cent in Serbia. Indeed, in two-thirds (67%) of the 36 nations, most of the non-agricultural workforce have their main job in the informal

Table 3.2 Extent of employment in the informal economy (by country)

Country	Year of survey	Employment in informal economy as % of all non-agricultural employment
Serbia	2010	6.5
Macedonia	2010	12.8
Moldova Republic	2009	15.9
Armenia	2009	19.8
South Africa	2010	32.7
China	2010	34.4
Brazil	2009	42.3
Uruguay	2009	43.7
Panama	2009	44.0
Costa Rica	2009	48.2
Venezuela	2009	48.2
Dominican Republic	2009	48.8
Argentina	2009	50.0
Mexico	2009	54.3
West Bank & Gaza	2010	59.0
Liberia	2010	60.3
Ecuador	2009	61.3
Colombia	2010	61.5
Sri Lanka	2009	62.1
Tanzania	2005/6	66.7
El Salvador	2009	68.2
Viet Nam	2009	68.5
Nicaragua	2009	69.4
Peru	2009	70.7
Paraguay	2009	70.7
Lesotho	2008	70.7
Indonesia	2009	72.4
Uganda	2010	73.5
Madagascar	2005	73.7
Honduras	2009	75.3
Bolivia	2006	75.6
Zambia	2008	76.3
Pakistan	2009/10	81.3
Philippines	2008	84.0
India	2009/10	84.3
Mali	2004	84.7

Source: derived from ILO (2012)

economy, meaning that the number with their main job in the informal economy outnumber those with their main job in the formal economy. There is, however, significant variation between countries.

Given these findings concerning the cross-national variations in the level of employment in the informal economy, our attention now turns towards evaluating critically the competing explanations for these variations.

3. Analysis: evaluating competing explanations for the cross-national variations in the size of the informal economy

Until now, as the last chapter revealed, there have been four competing explanations for the cross-national variations in the scale of employment in the informal economy. To select the indicators for evaluating the competing explanations, proxy indicators for the various tenets of each theorization are taken from the World Bank development indicators database for the year in which the survey was conducted in each country (World Bank 2013). The only indicators taken from non-official sources are on perceptions of public sector corruption, which have been taken from Transparency International's corruption perceptions index for the relevant year in each country (Transparency International 2013), the Human Development Index (HDI) and the Social Progress Index as a measure of "development" (Social Progress Imperative 2014; United Nations Development Programme 2014).

Beginning with the modernization explanation that the size of the informal economy is higher the less developed is the economy, the correlation between cross-national variations in participation in the informal economy and cross-national variations in GNP per capita is analysed across these 36 economies. Using Spearman's rank correlation coefficient, and as Figure 3.4 portrays, the finding is that there is a strong statistically significant relationship within a 99 per cent confidence interval ($r_s = -.520^{***}$). The direction of this relationship is that the level of participation in the informal economy is higher in economies with lower levels of GNP per capita. However, akin to previous studies reaching the same conclusion (ILO 2012; Yamada 1996), it is not possible to establish the direction of the correlation in terms of any cause-effect relationship. This, in consequence, is a limitation of both this and previous studies.

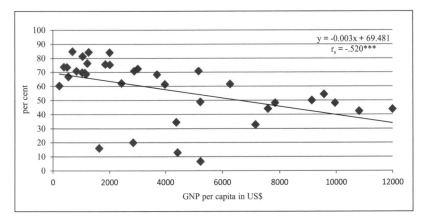

Figure 3.4 Relationship between participation in the informal economy and GNP per capita

In recent years, however, alternative indicators of the level of "development" have emerged which account for a wider range of variables other than simply economic productivity. Evaluating these measures of "development" more widely defined, a strong statistically significant correlation is identified between cross-national variations in the size of the informal economy and cross-national variations in not only household consumption expenditure per capita ($r_s = -.613$***) but also the Human Development Index ($r_s = -.497$***) and Social Progress Index ($r_s = -.509$***). Examining whether the scale of the informal economy is greater when public sector corruption is higher because this results in citizens exiting the formal economy in order to seek livelihoods beyond the corrupt public sector officials, a strong statistically significant association is identified between countries with higher perceived levels of public sector corruption and larger informal economies ($r_s = -.502$***). The informal economy therefore, across a range of indicators of "development", is higher in less developed economies, confirming the modernization theory.

Turning to the neoliberal explanation that employment in the informal economy is an outcome of higher tax rates, and interference by the state in the operation of the free market, analysis commences by testing several measures of taxation. Examining the relationship between the cross-national variations in the size of the informal economy and the level of taxes on goods and services as a percentage of revenue, a statistically significant correlation is identified (r_s = -.430***). However, its direction is the inverse of that suggested by neoliberals. The size of the informal economy decreases as taxes on goods and services increases. This, therefore, refutes a core tenet of neoliberal theory. Given this, two additional measures of taxation are here evaluated. Analysing cross-national variations in the level of revenue (excluding grants) as a share of GDP and cross-national variations in the size of the informal economy, a statistically significant association is identified (r_s = -.510***). Again, nevertheless, it is in the opposite direction expected by neoliberal theory. This is also the case when the association between cross-national variations in the level of tax revenue as a proportion of GDP and cross-national variations in the size of the informal economy are analysed. Once more a strong statistically significant association is found (r_s = -.451***), but in the opposite direction to what neoliberal theory states. On all three measures of tax rates, in sum, the size of the informal economy is lower in nations with higher tax rates. One reason that higher tax levels are correlated with smaller informal economies is that taxes provide the state with higher revenues to allow social transfers so that citizens receive social protection, thus reducing the necessity of the population to participate in the informal economy.

To evaluate the neoliberal tenet that state interference in the operation of the market leads to bigger informal economies, as well as the contrary political economy stance that the size of the informal economy reduces with greater state intervention, the relationship between cross-national variations in the size of the informal economy and the level of social contributions as a percentage of revenue can be analysed. A strong significant correlation is identified between the level of social contributions and the size of the informal economy (r_s = -.609***). The size of the informal economy reduces as social contributions rise as a share of revenue. This supports the political economy explanation that bigger informal economies are correlated with too little state intervention in the form of social protection. The neoliberal argument that state intervention leads to larger informal economy is not validated.

A similar finding is reached when other indicators of state intervention are investigated, namely state revenue as a share of GDP as well as the expense of government as a share of GDP. There is a steep decline in the size of the informal economy as state revenue as a share of GDP increases

(r_s = -.605***) as well as when the expense of government as a share of GDP increases (r_s = -.555***). Bigger government results in not an increase, but a decrease, in the size of the informal economy. Again, the neoliberal tenet that state interference leads to larger informal economies is therefore not validated. Instead, the political economy tenet is validated that higher levels of participation in the informal economy is associated with too little state intervention.

Finally, and turning to the political economy tenet that cross-national variations in the size of the informal economy are associated with necessity, a statistically significant relationship is identified between cross-national variations in the share of the population living below the national poverty line and participation in the informal economy (r_s = -.355*). The higher the proportion of the population living below the national poverty line, the larger is the informal economy, suggesting that the informal economy may well be a survival practice of marginalized groups used when no alternative means of livelihood or support are available, as asserted by the political economy explanation.

Finally, and evaluating institutional theory, a strong significant correlation is identified between trust in the legal system and the size of the informal economy (r_s = -.710***). The higher is the level of trust, the smaller is the informal economy. Seen from the perspective of third-wave institutional theory, therefore, the formal institutional imperfections that lead to the existence of institutional asymmetry and therefore the prevalence of the informal economy, are those structural determinants associated with the modernization and political economy explanations. These are namely that institutional asymmetry arises when there is a lack of economic development and modernization of government, and there is a lack of state intervention in both work and welfare provision and therefore greater deprivation.

Conclusions

This chapter has evaluated the methods used to measure the size of the informal economy, showing that not only can indirect measurement methods be used that draw upon statistical data collected for other purposes, but also direct survey methods that evaluate participation in the informal economy. Following this, two studies have been reported, with one reporting an evaluation of the size of the informal economy using an indirect measurement method and the other using a direct survey approach.

The first study, reporting the results of an indirect measurement method, estimates the size of the informal economy by evaluating the discrepancy between reported labour inputs from the supply-side (namely, labour force surveys) and reported labour inputs from the demand-side (namely business surveys). Based on the assumption that enterprises may try to hide labour inputs in the informal economy, the discrepancy is a measure of the informal economy. Using this labour input method (LIM) to evaluate the size of the informal economy across the European Union, the finding is that 9.3 per cent of total labour input in the private sector in the EU is in the informal economy, and that the informal economy constitutes 14.3 per cent of GVA in the private sector. There are, however, marked variations in the size of the informal economy across countries, ranging from 25 per cent of total GVA in Poland, Romania and Lithuania, to 7 per cent in Germany. Evaluating the different theoretical explanations of the informal economy, the finding is that the size of the informal economy is greater where there is institutional asymmetry, and that the formal institutional failures across the EU that are strongly associated with larger informal economies are weak GDP per capita, a lack of modernization of government and higher levels of corruption, a lack of state intervention in work and welfare, and greater inequality.

The second study reports the results of a direct survey of 36 developing countries. This again reveals that across all these developing countries, three out of every five (59.8%) non-agricultural workers have their main employment in the informal economy, although there are marked cross-national variations in the proportion of the workforce with their main job in the informal economy, ranging from 84.7 per cent of the non-agricultural workforce in Mali to 6.5 per cent in Serbia. Evaluating the contrasting theoretical explanations, it is again revealed that institutional asymmetry is strongly correlated with the size of the informal economy, and that the formal institutional failures across the developing world that are significantly associated with larger informal economies are again those proposed by modernization and political economy theory.

4

Characteristics of the informal economy

Introduction

What types of informal work exist? Who participates in the informal economy? Why do they do so? This chapter seeks answers to these questions regarding the characteristics of the informal economy. To do so, the first section introduces the different types of work in the informal economy, revealing how over recent decades a plethora of heterogeneous forms of work have been recognized to exist in the informal economy. Secondly, and to analyse who engages in the informal economy, the widely-held marginalization thesis is evaluated which holds that it is groups marginalized from the formal labour market who are more likely to participate in the informal economy. Thirdly, the reasons for participation in the informal economy are evaluated. This will analyse whether it is indeed the case that the participation of workers in the informal economy is largely necessity-driven due to their exclusion from the formal economy and alternative means of livelihood, or whether at least some workers participate in the informal economy because they desire to exit the formal economy, perhaps due to the level of public sector bribery and corruption they witness when seeking to work in the formal economy. Having reviewed who supplies informal work and their reasons for doing so, the fourth section then turns to the demand-side and evaluates who purchases goods and services in the informal economy and their motives for doing so. Whether goods and services are purchased in the informal economy solely due to them being cheaper, or whether other reasons for doing so also prevail, will be examined in the context of a case study of the 28 countries of the European Union. Finally, some conclusions will be drawn about the character of the informal economy in terms of what it is, who participates and why they do so.

Types of informal work

During the latter half of the twentieth century until around the 1980s, a widely-held view was that work in the informal economy was low-paid waged employment conducted under "sweatshop-like" exploitative conditions in which legislation on health and safety standards, minimum wages, holiday entitlements, working hours and so on, did not apply. Over the past few decades, however, it has been recognized first, that work in the informal economy can be also conducted on a self-employed basis and secondly, and more recently, that much of this own-account work is not always conducted for profit and can be also conducted by and for close social relations such as family, friends, neighbours and acquaintances as "paid favours". In what follows we shall examine what is known about each form of informal work.

Informal waged employment

For many decades, work in the informal economy was widely assumed to be exploitative low-paid employment conducted by marginalized populations out of necessity, as a survival strategy (e.g. Castells & Portes 1989; Davis 2006; Sassen 1997). Jobs in the informal economy were viewed as existing at the bottom of a hierarchy of types of employment, with workers receiving low wages, few benefits, and suffering poor working conditions (Castells & Portes 1989; Gallin 2001). The resultant belief was that the informal economy had near enough entirely negative consequences for governments, workers, businesses and consumers (see Chapter 1). Although it has now been recognized that the majority of informal work is conducted on an own-account basis, it is important that the existence of such exploitative waged employment is not forgotten or ignored.

Informal waged employment when conducted by marginalized populations is often low-paid sweatshop-like work conducted for unscrupulous employers, such as under conditions of forced labour (Davis 2004). In the English Localities Survey conducted in the late 1990s, for example, many instances were identified of waged informal employment conducted by residents of deprived urban neighbourhoods in England, and in nearly all instances the wage rates were below the national minimum wage (£3.60 at the time). Examples identified included: doing bar work for two weeks for

£50; working in a restaurant for £2.00 per hour; working early mornings in a small bakery for £20 per month; working full-time for three weeks in a canteen on a building site for £50; being paid £10 to clean trucks for 3 hours; staffing an ice-cream stall for £2.80 per hour and refurbishing a pub for one week for £100. In 90 per cent of these cases, it was unemployed people who undertook such work and their sole rationale was that they needed the money. In total, however, this waged employment accounted for just 2 per cent of all paid informal work in these lower-income populations (Williams & Windebank 2001).

This wholly informal waged employment, however, is not the only form of waged informal employment. Besides such unregistered employment where the employee is not registered as an employee, there also exists waged informal employment that challenges the conventional formal/informal binary divide. Over the past decade, a small but growing literature has drawn attention to how formal employers often reduce their tax and social security payments and therefore their labour costs by paying their formal employees two salaries: an official formal salary and an additional informal ("envelope") wage which is hidden from the tax and social security authorities. The instigation of this illegal labour practice usually occurs at the job interview stage. Alongside the agreement to pay an official formal wage detailed in a formal written contract, the employer at the same time reaches a verbal unwritten agreement with the employee to pay an additional "envelope wage" not declared to the tax and social security authorities (Williams 2009; Woolfson 2007). This salary under-reporting thus arises from fraudulent labour contracts where additional verbal conditions are requested by the employer that differ from the conditions enshrined in the written contract. Unless the employee agrees to these conditions, then generally they do not get the job. These additional conditions imposed in the verbal contract may include: that the employee will not take their full statutory entitlement to annual leave; that they will work longer hours than stated in their formal contract (which often means working more than the maximum hours in the working hours directive and/or being paid less than the minimum hourly wage), and/or that they will have different tasks and responsibilities to those specified in their formal contract (Williams 2014a, 2014b). This verbal contract supersedes the formal written contract of employment in that it constitutes the unwritten "psychological contract" regarding their conditions of employment. Although verbal agreements in many countries are legal and hold the same weight in law as a written contract, this verbal contract to under-report salaries is illegal because it fraudulently under-reports the wage earned by the employee in order to evade the full tax and social security payments owed by the employee and employer.

Since the turn of the millennium, research has revealed how formal employers in Central and Eastern European nations often seek to reduce their tax and social security payments and thus labour costs by paying their formal employees such an additional "envelope wage". This has been identified in studies conducted in Estonia (Merikūll & Staehr 2010), Latvia (Merikūll & Staehr 2010; Sedlenieks 2003; Žabko & Rajevska 2007), Lithuania (Karpuskiene 2007; Merikūll & Staehr 2010; Woolfson 2007), Romania (Neef 2002), Russia (Williams & Round 2007b) and Ukraine (Williams 2007).

A 2013 Eurobarometer survey of 11,025 employees in 28 European countries, revealed that one in 33 employees receive under-reported salaries, mostly from small businesses, and such a wage payment is more common with vulnerable employee groups (e.g. unskilled workers, with lower education levels and financial difficulties). It is important to point out, moreover, that this illegal wage practice of paying a formal employee an additional informal "envelope wage" is not confined to East-Central Europe. It is also prevalent in Western Europe and Nordic nations. The difference is that in East-Central Europe a portion of the regular salary of formal employees is paid as an envelope wage, whereas in Western Europe and Nordic countries, it is more commonly paid for overtime or extra time worked by a formal employee (Williams & Horodnic 2017).

Informal self-employment

Over the past twenty years, it has become increasingly recognized that there is a continuum of forms of informal work ranging from wholly informal waged employment conducted by employees for a business at one end, to wholly informal self-employment at the other (Williams 2004c). This recognition that informal work can be conducted on a self-employed basis has resulted in a more positive depiction of the informal economy as a hidden enterprise culture (Williams 2006a; Williams *et al.* 2016). Indeed, based on this, a new sub-discipline of entrepreneurship scholarship has emerged that seeks to understand the nature of informal entrepreneurship (Adom & Williams 2012; Coletto & Bisschop 2017; De Castro *et al.* 2014; Harris-White 2017; Khan 2017; Mesic 2016; Ostapenko & Williams 2016; Sasaki *et al.* 2016; Sauka *et al.* 2016; Slack *et al.* 2016; Thai & Turkina 2014; Villaries-Varela *et al.* 2017; Webb *et al.* 2009, 2010, 2013; Williams 2013d, 2014a, 2014b, 2015c, 2016, 2017; Williams & Gurtoo 2017b; Williams & Nadin 2010).

A more positive view has consequently emerged that the informal economy is one of the main breeding grounds for enterprise creation and a crucible where business start-ups test-trade the viability of their business venture before deciding whether to establish a formal enterprise (Copisarow 2004; Copisarow & Barbour 2004; Dellot 2012; Katungi *et al.* 2006; Llanes & Barbour 2007; Small Business Council 2004; Williams 2006a, 2010a; Williams *et al.* 2011, 2012a, 2012b). This view has had a major influence on public policy. The conventional approach that sought to eradicate the informal economy is now widely believed to eliminate with one hand of government precisely the entrepreneurship that other hands of government so desperately wish to nurture (Small Business Council 2004). The outcome has been that tax administrations and labour inspectorates across the world have begun to move away from their conventional approach of eradicating this "hidden enterprise culture" and instead shifted towards an enabling approach that has sought to develop policy measures to facilitate the formalization of such ventures (Dekker *et al.* 2010; ILO 2015; OECD 2012; Williams 2017; Williams & Nadin 2012a, 2012b, 2013a, 2013b; Williams & Renooy 2013). Indeed, this has become enshrined in policy with ILO Recommendation 204 advocating the formalization of the informal economy, rather than its eradication (ILO 2015).

What, however, is the evidence that businesses start-up in the informal economy and do so to test-trade the viability of their business? In 2012, a YouGov survey, funded by the Royal Society of Arts, of 595 owners of small businesses in the UK was undertaken. Some 55 per cent reported that trading in the informal sector was necessary when starting a business and 20 per cent (1 in 5) reported that they did so when starting their own business, and for two-thirds (64%), their main reason was to test the viability of the business venture. Examining the 13 per cent of all businesses who start-up in the informal economy to test-trade their venture, multivariate analysis reveals that businesses started by men, with low current annual turnovers and in specific sectors are significantly more likely to do so. Regional variations are not significant (Williams & Martinez 2014d). More than 1 in 8 formal businesses interviewed, therefore, used the informal economy as an incubator (i.e. they operate unregistered and trade informally to test-trade the viability of their enterprises). This is a significant minority of all small business start-ups. However, more than double the number of businesses started by men (just over 1 in 6) than by women (just over 1 in 14) test-traded in the informal economy. The reason it is lower for women is because they see their entrepreneurial endeavour more as a "hobby" or "side-line" and not as a "real business" venture in the initial stages (Williams & Martinez 2014e).

The English Localities Survey conducted in the late 1990s, meanwhile, evaluated the extent to which participants had engaged in enterprising activities and whether this was in the informal economy. As I have shown elsewhere (Williams 2008), some 23 per cent of entrepreneurs were found to start-up on an unregistered basis trading wholly in the informal economy, akin to the 2012 YouGov survey (Williams & Martinez 2014). The results of interviews in higher- and lower-income urban and rural English localities with 91 early-stage entrepreneurs (Williams 2010) reveal that their preponderance to trade informally is greater in lower-income and rural localities. In affluent urban and rural areas, that is, some 58 per cent and 62 per cent of early-stage entrepreneurs, respectively, trade informally, but 84 per cent and 87 per cent in lower-income urban and rural localities. There was thus a greater preponderance to start-up trading informally in lower-income populations.

In recent years, the evidence on this issue has markedly improved and there has been a global analysis of the proportion of businesses that start-up unregistered and operate in the informal economy. Autio and Fu (2015) find that two-thirds of businesses start-up without registration not only in developing and transition economies (where 0.62 unregistered businesses are created annually for every 100 people compared with 0.37 registered businesses) but also in OECD countries (where 0.62 unregistered businesses compared with 0.43 registered businesses are annually created for every 100 people). This provides evidence that if tax administrations and labour inspectorates were to seek to eradicate unregistered start-ups, then they would destroy some two-thirds of entrepreneurial ventures and thus the enterprise culture that governments so desperately want to nurture, as a means of pursuing economic development and growth. Indeed, it is precisely for this reason that governments across the world have shifted away from seeking the eradication of the informal economy and towards formalizing the informal economy (European Commission 2007, 2016; ILO 2015; OECD 2012).

One further insight regarding such entrepreneurial endeavour in the informal economy is that it is not always for-profit driven (i.e. commercial entrepreneurship), which for many years was the assumption. However, a series of recent studies has revealed that informal entrepreneurs range from purely rational economic actors pursuing for-profit logics through to social entrepreneurs pursuing solely non-commercial logics, with the majority somewhere in-between combining both for-profit and social rationales. The result has been a call for a more nuanced understanding of the heterogeneous logics of informal entrepreneurs that recognizes the existence of social entrepreneurs in the realm of informal entrepreneurship. Neither, furthermore, do informal entrepreneurs' logics remain static. The majority interviewed in studies in Ukraine, Russia and the UK state that their rationales had changed since starting up, and that roughly the same proportion had shifted away from commercial to more social rationales as the number who had shifted from social to more commercial rationales (Williams & Nadin 2011a, 2011b, 2012a, 2012b, 2012c).

Paid favours

A small body of research, furthermore, has highlighted how such informal self-employment or own-account work covers a spectrum of activities ranging from profit-motivated entrepreneurial endeavour, through social entrepreneurship, to smaller-scale, often one-off, paid favours conducted for close social relations such as neighbours, friends, or family (Cornuel & Duriez 1985; Jensen *et al.* 1996; Williams 2004c). One study of incomers to new towns in France, for example, found that participants often engaged in paid favours for their neighbours not to make money but to develop their social networks, to forge greater trust and the opportunity for reciprocity (Cornuel & Duriez 1985). Similarly, a study of rural Pennsylvania showed that many participating in informal work voiced reasons for doing so that had little or nothing to do with profit (Jenson *et al.* 1996).

By far the most extensive research on this issue, however, is in lower- and higher-income urban and rural neighbourhoods in England (Williams 2004c, 2009; Williams & Windebank 2001). It was identified that some 16 per cent of all informal work in higher-income districts was conducted for close social relations as paid favours, but 68 per cent in lower-income neighbourhoods. Moreover, over half of all community self-help in lower-income urban neighbourhoods is found to have become monetized, meaning that to deter paid favours would be to eradicate most of the active citizenship in such neighbourhoods (Williams 2003; Williams & Windebank 2001). Economic gain, moreover, hardly figured in their rationales. For example, a person may employ their cousin who is unemployed and in need of money to redecorate their living room in order to give them some money in a manner that avoids any connotation that "charity" is involved, which may result in the cousin refusing to accept the money. Similarly, a plumber or electrician may do some work at greatly reduced "mate's rates" for an elderly person or somebody in financial difficulties known to them who would otherwise be unable to afford to get some necessary repair work done. These redistributive and social network rationales are also evidenced in a study of women's undeclared work in Salford in the UK (Brill 2010), and a study of 134 persons in the small city of Limninge in Sweden which come to similar conclusions that most informal work is composed of paid favours for and by close social relations to help others out, such as when getting the car repaired (Larsen 2013a, 2013b).

Recent years have seen a further reinforcement of this finding that a large proportion of all informal work is conducted by and for close social relations as paid favours for redistributive and community-building purposes. The 2007 Eurobarometer survey of informal work, for example, reveals that 55 per cent of all informal work in the EU-27 is conducted for close social relations as "paid favours" (Williams & Renooy 2013) and the 2013 Eurobarometer survey shows that this figure has further increased during the economic crisis (European Commission 2013). In the UK in 2007, 60 per cent of all informal work was paid favours (Williams 2004c) and largely undertaken for reasons other than financial gain, such as to help others out. The result, and akin to the hidden enterprise culture discussed above, is that any attempt to deter or eradicate such paid favours will bring one sphere of government eradicating active citizenship into conflict with another part seeking to foster it.

Who works in the informal economy?

When work in the informal economy was solely viewed as exploitative waged employment, the perception was that such work is disproportionately conducted by marginalized groups. As a more nuanced understanding of the characteristics of work in the informal economy has emerged, this perception has been slow to change. It has continued to be the case that such work has been viewed as disproportionally conducted by, for example, populations living in marginalized areas. This applies whether discussing global regions (ILO 2012; Williams 2013d), cross-national variations (Schneider 2013; Schneider & Williams 2013; Williams 2015c), variations across localities (Kesteloot & Meert 1999; Williams & Windebank 2001) or urban–rural variations (Button 1984; Williams 2010c). A similar view exists when examining how participation in the informal sector varies by socio-demographic and socio-economic characteristics. For example, unemployed people are viewed as more likely to participate in the informal sector than those in formal jobs (Brill 2011; Castells & Portes 1989; Leonard 1994; Slavnic 2010; Taiwo 2013; Williams & Nadin 2014). Similarly, women are claimed to be more likely to participate in this realm than men (ILO 2013; Leonard 1994, 1998; Stănculescu 2004) and those with financial difficulties more likely than more affluent population groups (Barbour & Llanes 2013; Katungi *et al.* 2006; Williams 2004c).

Indeed, this view lies at the heart of both the modernization and political economy theses outlined in Chapter 2. For modernization theory, the informal sector is a leftover of a previous mode of production that persists in marginal enclaves that have not yet been subjected to modernization and economic development. The informal sector is thus viewed as typically conducted by, for example, uneducated people in small unproductive enterprises in separate "bottom of the pyramid" markets producing low-quality products for low-income consumers using little capital and adding little value (La Porta & Schleifer 2008, 2014).

For scholars adopting a political economy perspective, meanwhile, the advent of a deregulated open world economy has led to diminishing state involvement in social protection and economic intervention, which means that those excluded from the formal labour market and social protection are pushed into the informal sector as a survival strategy (ILO 2015; Meagher 2010; Taiwo 2013). Informal work therefore, is viewed in this political economy perspective as "necessity-driven" endeavour conducted by marginalized populations excluded from the formal labour market and social protection systems (Castells & Portes 1989; Gallin 2001; Williams & Round 2010).

However, this dominant view of informal work as disproportionately conducted by marginalized populations has started to be contested. Based on the view that necessity is not the only factor driving populations to engage in informal work, it has been argued that it is not always marginalized populations who engage in informal work. Indeed, several studies reveal that informal work is more prevalent in affluent regions and localities (Evans *et al.* 2006; van Geuns *et al.* 1987; Williams 2004a; Williams & Windebank 2001). Similarly, it has been sometimes asserted that unemployed people are less likely to participate than people who have formal jobs (MacDonald 1994; Pahl 1984; Renooy 1990; Williams 2001). This is the case for at least four reasons: (1) they lack the resources (such as car, tools) necessary to engage in a wide range of informal work (Pahl 1984; Williams 2004b); (2) they receive and hear about fewer opportunities to do so due to their smaller and more confined social networks (Komter 1996; Morris 1994; Williams 2006b); (3) they lack the skills and competencies to conduct informal work (Fortin *et al.* 1996; Renooy 1990) since if their skills and competencies are inappropriate for finding formal employment, there is no reason to believe that they are appropriate for finding informal work either; and (4) they fear being reported to the authorities, not least because claiming welfare benefits illicitly is popularly considered a more serious offence than tax evasion (Cook 1997; Williams 2004b, 2014). It has also been asserted that women are less likely to participate in informal work than men (Lemieux *et al.* 1994; McInnis-Dittrich 1995) and those with financial difficulties less likely to participate than more affluent population groups (Williams 2004c; Williams *et al.* 2013).

This questioning of whether the informal sector is concentrated amongst the marginalized arises out of two agency-oriented theorizations. On the one hand, a rational economic actor perspective has depicted informal workers as rational actors who, after weighing up the costs of informal work and benefits of formality, decide not to operate in the formal economy. For these scholars, burdensome regulations, high taxes and corruption among public sector officials lead people to voluntarily exit the formal sector and to operate informally (De Soto 1989, 2001; Nwabuzor 2005). On the other hand,

and drawing inspiration from institutional theory (North 1990), another agency-oriented group of scholars adopting a more "social actor" approach, view informal work as illegal but socially legitimate endeavour that arises when the formal institutions are not in symmetry with the norms, values and beliefs that constitute the informal institutions (De Castro *et al.* 2014; Kistruck *et al.* 2015; Siqueira *et al.* 2014; Thai & Turkina 2014; Webb *et al.* 2009, 2013, 2014). When there is symmetry between formal and informal institutions, informal work only occurs unintentionally such as due to a lack of awareness of the laws and regulations. When there is institutional asymmetry however, the result is more informal work. Indeed, the greater the degree of asymmetry, the greater is the level of informal work (Williams & Shahid 2016).

To evaluate whether marginalized populations are more likely to participate in the informal economy, let us examine a survey of the 28 member states of the European Union (EU28) involving 27,563 face-to-face interviews undertaken in 2013 (European Commission 2014b). This found that the most affluent European region, namely the Nordic nations, has the highest participation rate in informal work (6 per cent) compared with 4 per cent in East-Central Europe, 4 per cent in Western Europe and 3 per cent in Southern Europe. This therefore negates the view that poorer European regions have higher participation rates in informal work. This is further reinforced when average earnings are examined. Those living in Nordic nations earn on average €511 from their informal work compared with €459 in East-Central Europe, €489 in Southern Europe and €391 in Western Europe. As such, affluent European regions have higher participation rates in informal work than less affluent European regions and earn more from such work.

Turning to socio-demographic, socio-economic and other forms of spatial variation, Table 4.1 displays that, contrary to the view that informal work is concentrated in marginalized groups, participation in informal work is higher amongst men than women (5 per cent of men participated in informal work over the past 12 months but only 3 per cent of women) and women earn 77 per cent less than men from such work. Furthermore, the unemployed are no more likely to participate in informal work than the employed and even when they do, their earnings are 86 per cent of the amount earned by the employed. Neither do respondents living in rural areas participate in informal work more than respondents living in urban areas. The tentative

Table 4.1 Participation in informal work in the EU, by socio-demographic, socio-economic and spatial characteristics

		% engaged in informal work	Mean
Gender	men	5	459
	women	3	355
Age	15–24	7	367
	25–34	6	447
	35–44	3	509
	45–54	4	478
	55–64	2	503
	65+	1	417
Marital status	married/remarried	2	420
	unmarried/cohabitating	7	406
	unmarried/single	6	411
	divorced/separated	5	451
	widowed/other	2	412
Social class	working class	4	437
	middle class	3	436
	higher class	3	167
	other/none	9	392
Age education ended	<15	3	412
	16–19	4	418
	20+	3	439
	still studying	7	358
Adults in household	1	4	442
	2	3	441
	3	4	349
	4+	4	400
Children	<10 years old	5	513
	10–14 years old	5	387
	<10 and 10–14	4	245
	no children	3	400
Employment	unemployed	4	383
	employed	4	442
Difficulty paying bills	most of the time	8	391
	from time to time	4	461
	almost never/never	3	393
Area	rural area or village	4	422
	small or middle-sized town	4	431
	large town	4	381

Source: author's calculations based on special Eurobarometer survey, no. 204 (2013)

suggestion from these descriptive statistics therefore, is that when examining gender, employment status and the urban/rural divide, participation is not greater among women, the unemployed and rural areas.

However, when examining other population groups, participation does appear to be greater among those seen as more likely to be marginalized. Not only are younger age groups more likely to participate in informal work, but so too those who are unmarried compared with married/remarried participants, those self-defining themselves as working class compared with those defining themselves as middle class or higher class, those with children, and those who have difficulty paying bills compared with those who seldom have difficulties. For all these population groups, participation in informal work is greater.

Analysing these descriptive statistics, the tentative conclusion is that it is not possible to assert that those participating in informal work are across all spatial, socio-demographic and socio-economic characteristics positively associated with the marginalized. To analyse whether these findings remain the same when other variables are held constant, Table 4.2 presents the results of a multilevel mixed-effects logistic regression (Snijders & Bosker 2012). To analyse the effect of the socio-demographic, socio-economic and spatial various independent variables on participation in informal work when other variables are held constant, an additive model is used. The first stage model (M1) includes solely the socio-demographic factors to examine their effects while the second stage model (M2) adds socio-economic factors alongside the socio-demographic factors, and the third stage model (M3) adds spatial factors to the socio-demographic and socio-economic factors to examine their influence on participation in informal work. Table 4.2 reports the results.

Model 1 in Table 4.2 shows that younger age groups are significantly more likely to participate in the informal economy, doubtless due to their greater exclusion from the formal economy (European Commission 2014a), as are those defining themselves as working class and single-person households, both of which might be explained in terms of the greater financial difficulties they often face. In addition, those whose values do not adhere to the formal rules and are more tolerant of informal work are more likely to participate in the informal economy, providing support for institutional theory. Those marginalized in the sense that their norms, values and beliefs regarding informal work do not conform to the formal rules are more likely to participate in such work (Williams & Martinez 2014a, 2014b).

Table 4.2 Multilevel mixed-effects logistic regression of participation in informal work

Variable	Model 1	Model 2	Model 3
Gender (CG: women):			
men	0.688*** (0.0669)	0.756*** (0.0682)	0.757*** (0.0682)
Age (CG: 15–24):			
25–34	−0.268** (0.127)	−0.267** (0.127)	−0.262** (0.127)
35–44	−0.659*** (0.139)	−0.645*** (0.139)	−0.644*** (0.139)
45–54	−0.801*** (0.142)	−0.783*** (0.142)	−0.791*** (0.142)
55–64	−1.094*** (0.157)	−1.108*** (0.158)	−1.118*** (0.158)
65+	−1.974*** (0.182)	−2.012*** (0.190)	−2.023*** (0.190)
Marital status: (CG: married/remarried)			
cohabitating	0.0894 (0.104)	0.0670 (0.105)	0.0659 (0.105)
single	−0.0872 (0.115)	−0.136 (0.116)	−0.135 (0.116)
divorced/separated	0.326** (0.131)	0.247* (0.132)	0.249* (0.132)
widowed	−0.231 (0.163)	−0.257 (0.165)	−0.259 (0.165)
Social class (CG: working class)			
middle class	−0.313*** (0.0723)	−0.166** (0.0754)	−0.154** (0.0757)
higher class	−0.519*** (0.237)	−0.283 (0.238)	−0.257 (0.239)
other/none	0.0392 (0.227)	−0.132 (0.236)	−0.126 (0.236)
Age stopped full-time education (CG: 15-years):			
16–19	−0.0654 (0.117)	0.0311 (0.119)	0.0217 (0.119)
20+	−0.0869 (0.128)	0.0715 (0.131)	0.0661 (0.131)
still studying	−0.176 (0.173)	−0.146 (0.180)	−0.142 (0.181)
Number 15+ years in household (CG:1 person):			
2 persons	−0.336*** (0.106)	−0.329*** (0.106)	−0.330*** (0.107)
3 persons	−0.254** (0.117)	−0.220* (0.117)	−0.222* (0.118)
4+ persons	−0.340*** (0.128)	−0.302** (0.129)	−0.300** (0.130)

Number of children: (CG: no children)			
children <10	-0.0239 (0.0998)	-0.0771 (0.101)	-0.0884 (0.101)
children 10–14	-0.0326 (0.127)	-0.0741 (0.128)	-0.0824 (0.128)
one or more <10 and 10–14	-0.0273 (0.153)	-0.110 (0.155)	-0.136 (0.155)
Tax morality	0.385*** (0.0169)	0.377*** (0.0171)	0.375*** (0.0171)
Employment (CG: unemployed):			
Employed		-0.204** (0.0835)	-0.203** (0.0835)
Difficulty paying bills last year (CG: most of the time)			
from time to time		-0.472*** (0.0930)	-0.484*** (0.0931)
almost never/never		-0.856*** (0.0990)	-0.883*** (0.0991)
Area respondent lives (CG: rural area or village):			
small/middle sized town			-0.0774 (0.0780)
large town			-0.113 (0.0859)
EU region: (CG: Western Europe)			
Southern Europe			-0.747** (0.316)
East-Central Europe			0.0701 (0.258)
Nordic nations			0.768** (0.377)
Constant	-3.447*** (0.249)	-2.933*** (0.261)	-2.802*** (0.302)
Observations	24,173	23,920	23,905
Number of groups	28	28	28
Random-effects parameters			
Identity: country			
Variance (constant)	0.372***	0.440***	0.275***

Note: Standard errors in parentheses ***p<0.01, **p<0.05, *p<0.1

Source: author's calculations based on special Eurobarometer survey, no. 204 (2013)

However, men are significantly more likely to participate in the informal economy than women, reflecting how the exclusion of women from the formal economy is further compounded when examining the informal economy. There is no significant correlation with participation in the informal economy and the age participants stopped education, or the number of children in the household. There is no correlation with marital status, other than amongst widowed/separated people who are more likely to participate than married/remarried people, again doubtless because they may need to participate in informal work to make ends meet and do so in ways not traceable by the authorities, such as for matrimony payments. This would suggest that a variegated understanding of the validity of the relationship between marginalization and participation in the informal economy is required. Participation is greater among some marginalized population groups (such as younger people, those defining themselves as working class, single-person households and those with non-conformist attitudes), but not others (such as women, the less educated).

When Model 2 adds the socio-economic factors of employment status and financial circumstances, there are no major changes to the influence of the socio-demographic variables on participation in the informal economy. The socio-demographic characteristics statistically significant in Model 1 remain the same. However, the additional finding is that the unemployed and those with financial difficulties are significantly more likely to participate in the informal economy than those with formal jobs and fewer financial problems. This therefore supports the view that marginalized groups are more likely to participate in the informal economy.

When spatial factors are added in Model 3, the significance of the socio-demographic and socio-economic characteristics remain the same. However, although no evidence exists that those living in rural areas participate more compared with those living in more urban areas, those living in the more affluent EU region of the Nordic nations are more likely to participate in the informal economy than those living in Western Europe, and those living in Southern Europe are less likely. As such, when considering the urban–rural divide and European regional variations, it is not marginal populations who participate more in the informal economy. At a European regional level, the informal economy is more prevalent in economies where the formal economy is stronger, not least because more money is in circulation that can be used to purchase goods and services from informal work.

In sum, younger age groups are significantly more likely to participate in the informal economy, as are those who are divorced/separated, those defining themselves as working class, the unemployed, single-person households, those more tolerant of informal work (who are marginalized in the sense that their values and attitudes do not conform to those of the codes, regulations and laws of the formal institutions) and those who have difficulties paying household bills. However, men are found to be significantly more likely to work informally than women, as are those living in the more affluent EU region of the Nordic nations. No significant relationship exists moreover, so far as the educational level, the number of children in the household or the urban–rural divide are concerned.

A variegated interpretation of the relationship between participation in informal work and marginalization is therefore required: some marginalized groups are more likely, but others are not.

Why do people work in the informal economy?

When work in the informal economy was viewed as low-paid and exploitative waged employment conducted by marginalized populations, the motive for engaging in such work was economic necessity. Such work was viewed as a survival strategy in the absence of alternative means of livelihood and workers as participating in the informal economy due to their exclusion from the formal economy (Castells & Portes 1989). However, the recognition that not all informal work is exploitative waged employment, and that a diverse array of socio-demographic groups engage in informal work, means that this notion that informal work is always and everywhere conducted out of necessity has been put under the spotlight.

In this section, we begin by examining some results of a study of the motives for participation in the informal economy in Europe, which serves to reveal the contrasting reasons for working in the informal economy. We then unpack the motives of those who engage in specific types of informal work, by looking at a study of the motives for providing paid favours, and finally, we examine a study of the motives of those engaged in entrepreneurial endeavour in the informal economy in urban Brazil. These studies reveal the need to move beyond the conventional depiction of informal work as always and everywhere conducted out of economic necessity and to develop more nuanced understandings of the motives for engagement in this sphere.

Motives for participation in the informal economy: a case study of Europe

As we have seen, when explaining participation in the informal economy, scholars have adopted either the political economy perspective that views workers as participating in the informal economy due to their "exclusion" from the formal labour market and state benefits (Davis 2006; Gallin 2001; Taiwo 2013) or a view that informal workers voluntarily "exit" the formal realm, with neoliberals portraying this as a rational economic decision (De Soto 1989, 2001; Maloney 2004; Perry & Maloney 2007) and institutionalist theorists portraying them more as social actors who reject the codified laws and regulations (Cross 2000; Gerxhani 2004; Snyder 2004).

Before we evaluate the European case-study of workers' motives, we will review these competing "exit" and "exclusion" explanations, and the literature that has sought to synthesize them by proposing that the informal economy is composed of a dual labour market composed of an exit-driven "upper tier" and an exclusion-driven "lower-tier" of informal workers.

Participation in the informal economy: a product of exclusion or exit?

For political economy scholars, the informal economy is a by-product of the shift towards a deregulated global economy (Castells & Portes 1989; Davis 2006; Slavnic 2010). On the one hand, the informal economy is an efficient "strategy used by firms – both large and small – to cut costs, improve competitiveness, and guarantee flexibility in firm management and employment" (Rakowski 1994b: 504). On the other hand, those no longer required by capitalism are off-loaded into the informal economy. Informal work is thus prevalent in excluded populations who conduct such work out of necessity as a survival tactic (Castells & Portes 1989; Sassen 1997). The informal economy provides income-earning opportunities for those excluded from the formal economy (Nelson & Bruijn 2005; Tokman 2001).

For other scholars, participation in the informal economy is a matter of choice rather than due to a lack of choice. Informal workers voluntarily "exit" the formal economy. On the one hand, this is asserted by neoliberals who view informal workers as making a rational economic decision to exit the formal economy (De Soto 1989, 2001; Maloney 2004; Perry & Maloney

2007). Participation in the informal economy is thus a populist reaction to over-regulation and a rational economic strategy of workers confronting high taxes and burdensome regulations (Maloney 2004; Packard 2007). On the other hand, scholars adopting institutional theory also view the informal economy as resulting from the formal economy but view those participating in the informal economy as social actors (Godfrey 2015; Webb *et al.* 2009; Williams & Horodnic 2015, 2016a, 2016b, 2016c). Informal work is viewed as activity occurring outside of formal institutional prescriptions but within the norms, values and beliefs of informal institutions (Godfrey 2011; Kistruck *et al.* 2015; Siqueira *et al.* 2016; Webb *et al.* 2009; Welter *et al.* 2015). It arises when formal institutional failings result in the laws and regulations not being in symmetry with the norms, values and beliefs of citizens, workers and employers (Webb & Ireland 2015; Webb *et al.* 2009; Williams & Horodnic 2015a). Indeed, the greater the degree of asymmetry, the higher is the level of informal work (Williams & Shahid 2016; Williams *et al.* 2016a, 2016b).

Although most scholars have adopted either an exit-driven or an exclusion-driven explanation for informal work (e.g. De Soto 2001; Snyder 2004), a small body of scholarship has transcended this dominant view that informal work is universally a result of either exit or exclusion. As Guillermo Perry and William Maloney (2007: 2) assert, "These two lenses, focusing, respectively, on informality driven by exclusion from state benefits and on voluntary exit decisions resulting from private cost-benefit calculations, are complementary rather than competing analytical frameworks". Based on this, the informal economy has been viewed as a dual labour market. As Gary Fields (1990, 2005) asserts, the informal labour market is composed of an "upper tier" of exit-driven informal workers and a "lower tier" of exclusion-driven informal workers. It has been asserted that exit-driven informal workers are more prevalent in developed countries and exclusion-driven informal workers in developing nations (Gërxhani 2004; Maloney 2004). Similarly, exclusion motives are asserted to be more common in relatively deprived populations and exit motives in relatively affluent groups (Gurtoo & Williams 2009; Williams *et al.* 2017). However, evaluations of the ratio of exit-driven to exclusion-driven participants in the informal economy have been notable by their absence. Neither have there been evaluations of the groups more likely to be in the exclusion-driven "lower tier" and exit-driven "upper tier".

Informal workers' motives in the European Union

Special Eurobarometer survey no. 402 (European Commission 2014b) on participation in informal work examines the motives for participation in informal work. Those deemed to adopt "exit" motives report at least one of the following reasons for their participation in the informal economy: bureaucracy or red tape for a regular economic activity overcomplicated; bureaucracy or red tape for minor or occasional activities overcomplicated; able to ask for a higher fee for work undertaken; both parties benefited; taxes and\or social security contributions too high; and "the State does not do anything for you, so why should you pay taxes". Meanwhile, those deemed to adopt "exclusion" motives report at least one of the following reasons: the customer insisted on the non-declaration; unable to find a regular job; informal working common practice in region/sector of activity so no real alternative; difficulty of living on social welfare benefits; and no other means of income available. Finally, those expressing "mixed" motives report at least one "exit" motive and at least one "exclusion" motive.

As Table 4.3 shows, 24 per cent of informal workers are solely exclusion-driven, 45 per cent are purely exit-driven and 31 per cent do so for a mixture of both exclusion- and exit-driven rationales. Those participating in informal work for purely exclusion-driven reasons in the European Union are therefore half the number of those doing so for purely exit-driven reasons.

However, the weight given to exit and exclusion rationales varies across European regions. To help analyse this, member states are here grouped into four EU regions: Western Europe (Austria, Belgium, France, Germany, Ireland, Luxembourg, Netherlands and the UK); East-Central

Table 4.3 Motives for working in the informal economy, by EU region (n = 1,048)

Region	Motives (%)		
	Exclusion	Exit	Mixed
European Union	24	45	31
Central & Eastern Europe	26	41	33
Western Europe	15	55	30
Southern Europe	43	22	35
Nordic nations	10	68	22

Source: author's calculations from special Eurobarometer no. 402 (2013)

Europe (Bulgaria, Croatia, Czech Republic, Estonia, Hungary, Latvia, Lithuania, Poland, Romania, Slovenia and Slovakia); Southern Europe (Cyprus, Greece, Spain, Italy, Malta and Portugal), and the Nordic countries (Denmark, Finland; Sweden). As Table 4.3 shows, Southern Europe has a 2:1 ratio of those purely exclusion-driven compared with those purely exit-driven. Conversely, Nordic nations and Western Europe have a 6.8:1 ratio and 3.6:1 ratio respectively between those purely exit-driven and those purely exclusion-driven.

The result is that debates about whether participants in the informal economy are either exclusion- or exit-driven need to be transcended. Instead, a both/and approach is more appropriate which recognizes that the informal economy is a dual informal labour market which has an exit-driven upper tier and exclusion-driven lower tier.

To evaluate whether a similar dual informal labour market exists when specific forms of work in the informal economy are considered, we now turn our attention to two kinds of informal work. First, the motives for conducting paid favours are analysed and secondly, the motives for engaging in informal entrepreneurship.

Paid favours: exit- and/or exclusion-driven?

With the recognition that a large proportion of all informal work is conducted by and for close social relations as paid favours, a view has emerged that such informal work is commonly undertaken as a voluntary choice to help others out (Boels 2014; Brill 2010; Hodosi 2015; Purdam & Tranmer 2014; Ramas 2016; Spandler et al. 2014; Williams 2014a, 2014b).

To evaluate the motives of those who provide paid favours to others, Williams and Horodnic (2017) report the results of special Eurobarometer survey no. 402 conducted in 2013 across the 28 member states of the European Union (EU-28). Of the 27,563 face-to-face interviews conducted in the EU-28, some 3 per cent reported participating in informal work in the last 12 months. Of these, more than two-thirds (67.5%) reported that this informal work had been supplied as paid favours to friends, relatives or neighbours. Across the EU-28, therefore, the majority (over two-thirds) of informal work is conducted for close social relations. However, although 77.8 per cent of informal work is for close social relations in Western Europe and 76.4 per cent in Nordic nations, this falls to 63.3 per cent in East-Central Europe and 47.2 per cent in Southern Europe where informal work is more likely to be conducted as waged employment.

It is also the case that the informal work of men is more likely to be for close social relations (perhaps because women conduct such community exchange on an unpaid basis), as is the informal work of younger and older age groups compared with prime age workers, those living in rural areas, those in employment compared with the unemployed, and those who almost never have difficulties paying the household bills. This suggests, therefore, that doing paid favours is not largely the province of marginalized populations.

Table 4.4 reports the motives for providing paid favours. Across the EU-28, just 16 per cent of those providing paid favours do so out of necessity. Some 53 per cent voluntarily choose to provide paid favours and the remaining 31 per cent do so for a mixture of necessity-driven and voluntary rationales. However, although primarily a voluntary endeavour, the rationale of necessity was more common in Southern Europe and in East-Central Europe. Meanwhile, purely voluntary rationales were more common in Nordic nations and West European countries.

In sum, the finding is that when examining the motives for paid favours, there again appears to be an "upper tier" of participants engaging in such community endeavour as a matter of choice. These are significantly more likely to be those in formal employment, those with few financial difficulties and living in Nordic nations. There is also a "lower tier" of necessity-driven participants doing so as a coping strategy. These are significantly more likely to be the unemployed and those living in Southern Europe. Moreover, the

Table 4.4 Reasons for providing paid favours, by EU region (n = 722)

Region	Motives (%)		
	Necessity	Voluntary	Mixed
EU-28	16	53	31
East-Central Europe	17	47	36
Western Europe	10	58	32
Southern Europe	42	32	26
Nordic nations	5	76	19

Source: author's calculations from special Eurobarometer no. 402 (2013)

number of participants in the "upper tier" is more than triple the number in the "lower tier". However, this ratio significantly varies across European regions. Southern Europe has a 1.3:1 ratio of those purely necessity-driven compared with those doing so more as a matter of choice. Conversely, Nordic nations and Western Europe have a 15:1 ratio and 5.8:1 ratio respectively between those doing so out of choice and those who are necessity-driven.

Motives for informal entrepreneurship: a case study of urban Brazil

To evaluate the motives for entrepreneurship in the informal economy, we shall examine a household survey conducted in Brazil during 2003 by the Brazilian Institute for Geography and Statistics (IBGE, *Instituto Brasileiro de Geografia e Estadística*), which is the national census bureau. This survey of the urban informal sector (*Pesquisa Economia Informal Urbana*, ECINF) generates cross-section data representative of the urban self-employed and micro-firm owners (5 or fewer paid employees), excluding domestic workers. In total, 54,595 households were interviewed. Of the 40,235 individuals identified who reported being either self-employed or owners of micro-businesses, just 8 per cent reported paying taxes and/or making social security contributions. Here, we examine the results of the 37,016 who did report not paying either taxes and/or making social security contributions (i.e. informal entrepreneurs).

To evaluate whether informal sector entrepreneurs are driven by exclusion into informal sector entrepreneurship or voluntarily exit the formal economy, participants were asked which of the following ten reasons was their major motivation for starting their micro-enterprise: family tradition; unable to find a formal job; to supplement net income; opportunity presented by partner; experience in the area; promising business opportunity; a secondary job; allowed working time flexibility; and provided independence. Table 4.5 groups these reasons by whether they are exclusion or exit rationales for participating in informal sector entrepreneurship.

Less than half (48.7%) of informal sector entrepreneurs in urban Brazil cite exclusion rationales, such as their inability to find a formal job or inadequate income. For 45.5 per cent of informal sector entrepreneurs, participation is a choice, with 16.5 per cent stating that it was due to the independence they get from pursuing this type of work; due to their experience or skills

Table 4.5 Motives for starting informal sector enterprise in Brazil, 2003

% of informal entrepreneurs	All informal entrepreneurs	Sole traders	With employees
Exclusion rationales:	**48.7**	**52.2**	**23.7**
Unable to find a formal job	31.1	33.2	16.0
To supplement net income	17.6	19.0	7.7
Exit rationales:	**45.4**	**42.0**	**69.4**
Independence	16.5	15.4	24.3
Experience in the area	8.4	7.6	13.9
Family tradition	8.1	7.6	11.8
Promising business	7.4	6.8	11.3
Secondary job	2.1	2.0	3.0
Opportunity presented by a partner	1.0	0.6	4.2
Working time flexibility	1.9	2.0	0.9
Other reasons	5.8	5.7	6.6
No response	0.1	0.1	0.3

Source: author's calculations based on IBGE, Diretoria de Pesquisas, Coordenação de Trabalho e Rendimento, Economia Informal Urbana 2003

in the area (8.4%); that they are following a family tradition (8.1%); and because it represented a promising business opportunity (7.4%).

One half therefore engage in informal entrepreneurship due to their exclusion from the formal economy, and a half out of choice. This varies, however, by whether they are sole traders or employers with five or fewer employees. Some 52.2 per cent of informal sector sole traders are primarily doing so due to their exclusion from the formal economy, but only a quarter (23.7%) of informal sector entrepreneurs with five or fewer employees. Sole traders are therefore driven more by exclusion into informal sector entrepreneurship, whilst entrepreneurs with micro-businesses are driven more by exit rationales.

In sum, no single explanation is universally valid in relation to all informal entrepreneurs. It is only by combining both that a comprehensive explanation can be achieved. It is not an issue of whether one or the other is universally correct, but rather, the weight given to each explanation in a particular context which is important.

Why do people purchase goods and services in the informal economy?

Until now, most studies on the informal economy have adopted a supply-side perspective. Research focuses upon those working in the informal economy, examining the types of work they conduct (Williams 2014c, 2015d), the demographic and socio-economic characteristics of informal workers and businesses (Wallace & Latcheva 2006; Kukk & Staehr 2014; Putniņš & Sauka 2015), and their motives for working in the informal economy (Maloney 2004; Williams & Schneider 2016). Less attention is paid to the demand-side, namely consumers sourcing goods and services from the informal economy and their rationales for doing so.

This section examines the research available on who makes purchases in the informal economy and their motives for doing so. We begin by looking at potential explanations for consumers making purchases in the informal economy which variously portray such consumers as either rational economic actors seeking a lower price; social actors purchasing for social and/ or redistributive rationales, or as doing so due to the failures of formal sector provision. We then evalute the relevance of these explanations.

Explaining purchases in the informal economy

The dominant explanation is that those who operate in the informal economy are rational economic actors pursuing monetary gain. The origin of this approach lies in the classic work of Jeremy Bentham (Bentham 1788) whose utilitarian theory portrays citizens as rational actors weighing up the rewards and risks of activities and disobeying the law when the expected penalty and risk of detection is lower than the profits gained. In the early 1970s, Michael Allingham and Agnar Sandmo (1972) applied this utility maximizing view to the informal economy. Ever since, those supplying informal work have been widely portrayed as rational economic actors who do so for financial gain (Castells & Portes 1989; Gallin 2001; Davis 2006), whilst consumers purchasing from the informal economy are seen to be seeking to benefit from the cheaper prices (Fortin *et al.* 1996; Bajada 2002).

Over recent years, a social actor explanation has emerged. This views exchanges in the informal economy to be for social reasons rather than for profit-motivated logics (Nelson & Smith 1999; White & Williams 2010c). For example, close social relations are paid for doing an activity (e.g. gardening work) so that they can be given money (e.g. when the person supplying the activity is unemployed), in a way that avoids any notion that charity is involved, which may prevent the person from accepting the money (Kempson 1996). Purchases in the informal economy from close social relations are therefore more akin to mutual aid than a profit-motivated market transaction (Williams 2004c; Zelizer 2005).

A third explanation is that consumers purchase from the informal economy due to imperfections in the formal economy. Just as informal workers are argued to voluntarily exit the formal economy because of problems confronted when working formally, such as high tax levels and stifling regulations (De Soto 1989, 2001; Maloney 2004; Small Business Council 2004; Cross & Morales 2007; Perry & Maloney 2007), consumers are asserted to turn to the informal economy due to the failings of the formal economy. These failings can relate to the lack of availability or reliability of formal economy businesses (e.g. formal businesses may not be available to do various tasks or simply fail to turn up), the speed of provision and the quality of the goods and services provided. Unless the availability, speed and quality of provision in the formal economy are resolved, therefore, consumers will continue to turn to the informal economy.

European consumers' motives for making purchases in the informal economy

In order to evaluate the validity of these competing explanations, we can examine the reasons for purchasing goods and services in the informal economy in the EU as reported in special Eurobarometer 402, which found that in 2013, 12 per cent of citizens surveyed reported knowingly purchasing informal goods and services.

Do purchasers therefore buy goods and services in the informal economy to pay a lower price? Or are they social actors doing so for social or redistributive reasons? Or is it more due to the failings of the formal economy (i.e. the availability, speed and quality of the goods and services provided)? To answer these questions, consumers were asked "What made you acquire it from a source involving informal income, instead of acquiring it on the open market?". As Table 4.6 shows, seeking a lower price is the sole motive in only

Table 4.6 Reasons consumers purchase goods and/or services in the informal economy, by EU region

	EU-28	East-Central Europe	Western Europe	Southern Europe	Nordic nations
Lower price alone	34	30	30	44	34
Social and/or redistributive reasons alone	15	8	19	12	15
Poor formal provision alone	13	17	13	9	19
Mix of lower price & social and/or redistributive reasons	13	11	14	14	8
Mix of lower price & poor formal provision	13	19	11	12	16
Mix of social and/or redistributive reasons & poor formal provision	5	6	5	3	2
Mix of lower price, social and/or redistributive reasons & poor formal provision	7	9	8	6	6

Source: author's calculations from special Eurobarometer no. 402 (2013)

34 per cent of cases, one of several rationales in 33 per cent of informal purchases and not cited in the remaining 33 per cent of cases. Rationales other than a lower price, therefore, prevail in two-thirds of cases where consumers purchase from the informal economy.

In 15 per cent of all cases, social rationales are the sole reason, and in a further 25 per cent social rationales are combined with other reasons. Some 13 per cent of purchases in the informal economy are purely due to poor formal sector provision and 25 per cent combined poor formal sector provision with other rationales. Many acquire goods and services in the informal economy, in consequence, for reasons other than purely financial gain.

In the EU, in consequence, consumers' motives for acquiring goods and services in the informal economy cannot be explained using just one or other of these explanations. Instead, all need to be used. Nevertheless, the weight given to each will change in different contexts. As Table 4.6 shows, the rationale of a lower price is more common in Southern Europe (44%) but less common in East-Central Europe (30%) and Western Europe (30%). Social and/or redistributive rationales alone, meanwhile, is more frequently stated in Western Europe (19%) while formal sector failings are perhaps unsurprisingly more common as the sole reason in East-Central Europe (17%) but also in the Nordic nations (19%).

Explanations also vary across population groups. Consumers more likely to cite a lower price, and who are thus more susceptible to changes in the cost/benefit ratio, are younger people, men, and those with a lower tax morality. Consumers statistically less susceptible to changes in the cost/benefit ratio are single people, managers, and those who never or almost never face difficulties paying bills. Those purchasing in the informal economy to help someone (i.e. social and/or redistributive reasons) are significantly more likely to have low tax morality, to be single and a self-employed or manual worker. For those purchasing in the informal economy due to the imperfections of the formal economy, the first issue to examine is which consumers do so due to the lack of availability of the good or service on the regular market. These are significantly more likely to be consumers who have a higher tax morality, to be older, and in employment, including the self-employed, managers and other white-collar workers. Those purchasing in the informal economy because of the speed or quality of services available are significantly more likely to be those in employment and those in East-Central Europe.

In sum, this review of the behaviour and motives of consumers making purchases in this realm reveals the need to transcend one-dimensional explanations of consumer motives and to adopt a more nuanced understanding appreciative of the multifarious logics across different populations. What is certain, moreover, is that consumers do not purchase in the informal economy solely for financial gain.

Conclusions

This chapter has evaluated the characteristics of the informal economy. It has reviewed the different varieties of work in the informal economy, who does it and why they do it. We find that although early studies assumed that informal work was low-paid waged work conducted under "sweatshop" conditions, work in the informal economy ranges from various types of informal waged employment through varieties of informal self-employment to paid favours. Moreover, we find that all social groups engage in informal work, although some are more likely to do so (e.g. younger age groups, those with financial difficulties), and that motives for participating in the informal economy both as suppliers and consumers range from economic necessity through to voluntary choice. One major outcome is that there appears to be a dual informal labour market composed of a lower tier of necessity-driven informal workers and an upper-tier of informal workers who engage in the informal economy more out of choice. The proportion in each group varies in different contexts.

5

Policy options and approaches

Introduction

Having shown the multifarious forms of informal work, diverse population groups who participate and wide range of motives for participation, we now turn to the issue of tackling the informal economy. To do so, this chapter reviews each of the four possible hypothetical policy goals available to governments: taking no action; eradicating the informal economy; deregulating the formal economy; or formalizing the informal economy. In each case, the disadvantages and advantages of these policy options are reviewed. This will reveal that if no action is taken, the disadvantages far outweigh the advantages. Secondly, if eradicating the informal economy is pursued as the policy goal, the disadvantages again outweigh the advantages, as is also the case when deregulation of the formal economy is pursued. In consequence, this chapter will argue that formalizing the informal economy is the most viable policy goal. Indeed, this is also the conclusion of the supra-national agencies when considering what is to be done about the informal economy (European Commission 2016; ILO 2015; OECD 2016).

Given this goal of formalizing the informal economy, the second section of the chapter reviews the policy measures available for achieving this objective. This will set out two broad sets of policy measures. On the one hand, there are direct policy measures, which seek either to dissuade participation in the informal economy and/or to incentivize and encourage participation in the formal economy. To do so, measures are used that directly increase the costs and reduce the benefits of informality, as well as reduce the costs and increase the benefits of operating in the formal economy. The aim in doing so is to address the formal institutional failing, namely the powerlessness of formal institutions, which results in the greater prevalence of the informal economy. Using these direct policy measures on their own, however, does not tackle the other formal institutional failures and imperfections that produce institutional asymmetry and thus the greater prevalence of the informal economy.

On the other hand, and to address these other formal institutional failures that lead to institutional symmetry and to large informal economies, indirect policy measures can be used. These include a variety of process innovations across government that develop the perceived level of procedural and redistributive justice and fairness of government, to reduce institutional symmetry. They also include other indirect measures that address wider formal institutional failures, which Chapter 2 revealed are significantly associated with greater institutional asymmetry, such as increasing the level of regulation, tax revenue as a percentage of GDP and the expense of government as a percentage of GDP.

These two broad sets of policy measures are not either/or choices. Direct and indirect policy measures are not mutually exclusive. Given that each policy approach tackles a different set of formal institutional failings, both are required to tackle the informal economy. In the past decade or so, how these should be combined and sequenced has started to be addressed. The concluding section of this chapter will provide an overview of two different views on how this might occur. First, we review a responsive regulation approach, which temporally sequences these two sets of measures by starting with the indirect policy measures and if these do not have the desired effect on behaviour, then introducing incentives to bring about behaviour change, and only when all else fails, are deterrents used to elicit behaviour change. Secondly, we examine a "slippery slope" approach, which argues that compliance is greatest when both the power of authorities (achieved by using direct policy measures) and trust in authorities (achieved using indirect policy measures) is high. If either the power of, or trust in, authorities is low, then governments will find themselves on a slippery slope and the informal economy will be large. Reviewing the evidence base to support this approach, the chapter argues that this latter approach of concurrently combining direct and indirect policy measures is the best way forward for bringing about a formalization of the informal economy.

Potential policy objectives

Reviewing the possible policy objectives open to governments when tackling the informal economy, there are four hypothetical options. Governments can select to either: take no action; eradicate the informal economy; deregulate the formal economy; or formalize the informal economy. At first glance, some of these policy objectives may seem a little outlandish. However, all these policy objectives have been advocated by various scholars over the past few decades. As such, none can be rejected without evaluating their advantages and disadvantages.

Take no action

The first policy objective that might be pursued is to do nothing about the informal economy. The rationales for taking no action are that:

- If the informal economy is relatively small, the revenue-to-cost ratios of reducing the informal economy or formalizing informal work may not be cost effective;
- The informal economy is a test-bed out of which emerges a large proportion of new business ventures (Williams & Martinez 2014e), so this realm should be left alone; and
- The informal economy is in large part composed of paid favours for family, friends, neighbours and acquaintances which in market-oriented societies is a main vehicle for active citizenship, so this realm should be left alone in order that governments do not with one hand destroy precisely the active citizenship that with another hand it is seeking to foster. These paid favours, furthermore, may often constitute the initial monetary exchanges out of which people recognize the possibility that an entrepreneurial venture might be created, and which enables them to test out their idea for a business venture.

For these reasons, a potentially viable policy objective may be to take no action. However, doing so will mean that all the negative consequences for formal businesses and workers, informal enterprises and workers, their customers, governments and the wider society will remain intact. These negative consequences were summarized in Chapter 1.

Until now, and as Chapter 1 highlighted, there has been no rigorous evaluation of the magnitude of these positive and negative consequences. This lacuna in scholarship will need to be filled in future. Even if a rigorous evidence-base is lacking, nevertheless, the widespread normative consensus is that on balance, the negative consequences of doing nothing outweigh the positive consequences and it is therefore not a valid policy approach.

However, even if pursuing solely this policy objective is not viable, it should perhaps not be entirely dismissed. For example, it could be considered that doing nothing is relevant in relation to small-scale one-off odd-jobs conducted as paid favours to help close social relations. If pursued, moreover, this would free government resources in labour inspectorates and tax administrations to concentrate on larger-scale tax evasion by businesses. In consequence, even if it is not relevant in relation to all informal work, this policy objective may be applicable to certain *types* of informal work. Overall, however, the negative consequences across all stakeholders of pursuing a laissez-faire approach means that intervention in the informal economy is required. What form of intervention in the informal economy, therefore, is required? Three alternative policy options exist in this regard.

Deregulate the formal economy

One policy option might be to deregulate the formal economy. The logic for pursuing this objective can be found in the neoliberal theoretical explanation that depicts the informal economy to be the outcome of over-regulation (De Soto 1989, 2001; London & Hart 2004; Nwabuzor 2005; Small Business Council 2004). Viewed from this neoliberal perspective, informal workers are viewed largely as own-account workers voluntarily choosing to operate in the informal economy on a self-employed basis and are celebrated as heroes who are casting off the shackles of state over-regulation (e.g. Sauvy 1984; De Soto 1989). Informal workers are thus only breaking unfair rules and regulations imposed by what is perceived as an excessively intrusive state.

The objective is therefore to reduce taxes and cumbersome state regulations to free those in the formal economy from the constraints that supposedly force up labour costs and prevent flexibility, and act as a disincentive to those seeking to operate in the formal economy. As Castells and Portes (1989: 13) put it, "In an ideal market economy, with no regulation of any kind, the distinction between formal and informal would lose all meaning since all activities would be performed in the manner we now call informal". With fewer regulations, the distinction between formal and informal work would thus wither away so that the formal and informal economies would become inseparable since all activities would be performed in the manner now called "informal", although such activity would be "formal" since it would no longer be breaking any rules.

However, several problems exist with pursuing this policy goal of deregulating the formal economy. First, there is little evidence that reducing taxes and deregulating the formal economy reduces the size of the informal economy, as shown in Chapter 3. Secondly, even if deregulation were to lead to a reduction in the amount of so-called formal regulated work and a growth of what is now termed informal work, the outcome would likely be lower quality work and a levelling down rather than up of working conditions (Williams 2006a).

Importantly, nevertheless, even if pursuing solely this policy option is not viable, it is again the case that it might be applied in some limited instances. Deregulation, such as in the form of the simplification of compliance, can be a useful tool when helping businesses start-up on a formal basis from the outset. If the regulatory burden is high and complex for businesses, and simpler compliance is possible, then deregulation will play an important role in tackling this type and reason for informality. The deregulatory approach is not a viable option across the whole informal economy, however, because it would produce a levelling down rather than up of working conditions. It would be formality in the context of lower levels of social protection and fewer rules and regulations, such as in relation to occupational health and safety, working conditions and customer protection. In sum, even if deregulation were to reduce the magnitude of the informal economy, the impact would be doubtless a widening of inequalities and a deterioration of working conditions compared with more regulated countries.

Eradicate the informal economy

Another policy objective might be to eradicate the informal economy. At first glance, eradicating the informal economy seems a valid option. In recent decades, however, numerous problems have been found with the practicability and desirability of eradicating the informal economy. On the one hand, there is the practical problem of whether it can be achieved as well as how to do it. On whether it can be achieved, such a goal is based on the premise that government authorities can be sufficiently powerful to eradicate the informal economy. Whether this is the case in those global regions where the informal economy is most prevalent is questionable. The global regions where the informal economy is most prevalent have weak formal institutional environments. Whether the power of authorities can be sufficiently enhanced to make the eradication of the informal economy feasible, or even its significant reduction, is debateable. Indeed, even when advanced market economies have sought to do so, the problem governments have confronted is that beyond a certain point, the cost of eradicating the informal economy outweighs the benefits. There is a point, therefore, beyond which it is difficult to progress when seeking to eradicate the informal economy.

On how its eradication can be achieved, the conventional approach has been to view those operating in the informal economy as "rational economic actors" who evade compliance because the pay-off is greater than the expected cost of being caught and punished (Allingham & Sandmo 1972), and to seek to change the cost/benefit ratio confronting actual or likely participants by concentrating on the cost side and increasing the perceived or actual likelihood of detection and the penalties and sanctions for those caught (Grabiner 2000; Richardson & Sawyer 2001). This, therefore, seeks to elicit behaviour change using "sticks" to punish those engaged in "bad" behaviour. However, issues have been raised about the efficiency and effectiveness of this deterrence approach. Although some find that improving detection and/or penalties reduces the informal economy (De Juan *et al.* 1994; Slemerod *et al.* 2001), others identify that the informal economy grows (Bergman & Nevarez 2006; Murphy 2005). Indeed, some eminent scholars have even concluded that "it is not sensible to penalize illicit work with intensified controls and higher fines" (Schneider & Enste 2002: 192). This is because it alienates these informal workers and businesses, decreases their willingness to comply and reduces their belief in the fairness of the system, especially if the fines are too high and they are treated in ways they do not perceive as fair and just (Murphy 2005). It is not just the practical issue of whether it is feasible to eradicate the informal economy and how its eradication can in practice be achieved that results in questions being asked about the policy goal of eradication.

Eradication is also perhaps not desirable. If the eradication of the informal economy is sought, then not only may it be costly for governments to achieve, but in doing so, governments will destroy precisely the entrepreneurial endeavour and active citizenship that they are seeking to nurture and develop in order to promote economic development and growth, and social cohesion. The resulting challenge for government is to "join-up" its policies towards the informal economy with its wider policies towards entrepreneurship and active citizenship. There is also perhaps a need to join up its policy towards the informal economy with its wider policies on employment creation and social cohesion.

Importantly, however, even if pursuing solely eradication as a policy goal is not viable, it could be pursued in some circumstances. In situations where informal workers and informal businesses have been given every opportunity to formalize but do not, then governments must be able to punish those not complying. In these contexts, the tools of an eradication approach, including penalties and sanctions, are needed. On its own, however, the eradication approach is not perhaps viable since this policy approach often contradicts wider policy goals associated with harnessing entrepreneurship, active citizenship, social cohesion and fuller-employment.

Move informal work into the formal economy

A fourth and final policy option is to move informal work into the formal economy. Beginning with the potential disadvantages, a major one is that those starting businesses will no longer be able to undercut the competition and to test-trade in the informal economy when starting up (although the latter issue is not relevant if this approach recognizes that many business start-ups are on a journey to formalization and facilitates them to take this journey), and another major disadvantage is that customers will need to pay the full market price which might mean that the role of the informal economy in providing cheaper goods and services will no longer be available. The benefits of moving informal work into the formal economy, nevertheless, outweigh the costs. These benefits can be related to the various groups of the population with a stake in this matter, namely formal and informal businesses, informal workers, customers and the government.

For formal businesses, the benefits of moving informal work into the formal economy are that it eliminates the unfair competitive advantage of informal over formal enterprises (Andrews *et al.* 2011; Evans *et al.* 2006; Karlinger 2013; Renooy *et al.* 2004), and enables a "high road" rather than "low road" approach to be pursued by businesses whereby they move towards ever greater regulatory standards on corporate social responsibility and conditions of work such as health and safety and labour standards (OECD 2016; Williams & Windebank 1998; Williams *et al.* 2013).

For informal businesses, the benefits of moving work from the informal economy into the formal economy are that: they can escape being pressured into exploitative supply chain relationships with the formal sector (Gallin 2001; Williams & Windebank 1998); have the same levels of legal protection as formal businesses (Castells & Portes 1989; ILO 2002a; Williams & Windebank 1998); and overcome the structural impediments to their development and growth, such as gaining access to capital and being able to secure the advice and support available to formal businesses (ILO 2002; OECD 2016; Williams *et al.* 2013).

Informal workers, meanwhile, especially those living in poverty, benefit from shifting their work into the formal economy because they: gain access to health and safety standards in the workplace (Evans *et al.* 2006; Gallin 2001; ILO 2002; Williams & Lansky 2013); enjoy the same employment rights as formal workers (Evans *et al.* 2006); gain access to mortgages and credit since their pay is official and recognized by lending institutions (Leonard 1994; Williams 2007); benefit from greater job security (Williams 2018); can get an employer's reference (ILO 2002); gain access to other legal rights such as the minimum wage, tax credits and the working hours directive (Leonard 1994; Renooy *et al.* 2004; Williams & Windebank 1998); can build-up rights to the state pension and other contributory benefits, and access occupational pension schemes (Gallin 2001; ILO 2002); enjoy bargaining rights (ILO 2002; Williams & Lansky 2013); improve their ability to evidence their employability; and reduce their constant fear of detection and risk of prosecution (Grabiner 2000).

For customers of the informal economy, meanwhile, the advantages of moving work from the informal economy into the formal economy are that they: benefit from legal recourse if a poor job is done; have access to insurance cover; enjoy guarantees in relation to the work conducted, and benefit from greater certainty that health and safety regulations have been followed.

Finally, and for governments, the benefits of moving work from the informal economy into the formal economy are that it: increases the tax revenues for the state, including income tax, national insurance and VAT (Evans *et al.* 2006; Grabiner 2000; Williams 2004b; Williams & Windebank 1998); has beneficial knock-on effects by increasing the money available to governments to pursue social cohesion (Williams & Windebank 1998); results in improved trade union and collective bargaining (Gallin 2001); allows the creation of more formal jobs to enable societies to move closer to the goal of full-employment; enables a joining-up of the policy approach towards the informal economy with the policy approaches towards entrepreneurship and active citizenship (Dekker *et al.* 2010; European Commission 2007a; Renooy *et al.* 2004; Small Business Council 2004; Williams 2006a); improves regulatory control over the quality of jobs and services provided in the economy (Gallin 2001); and encourages a more positive attitude towards the law more widely (Renooy *et al.* 2004).

In sum, this brief review of the four policy objectives displays that the first goal of taking no action leaves intact the current disadvantages for formal entrepreneurs (e.g. unfair competition), informal entrepreneurs (e.g. the inability to gain access to credit to expand), customers (e.g. no guarantee of health and safety standards) and governments (e.g. taxes owed are not collected). The second goal, eradicating the informal economy, would result in governments repressing exactly the entrepreneurship and active citizenship that they wish to foster, and the third goal, deregulating the formal economy, would level down rather than level up working conditions. Transferring informal work into the formal economy is consequently the most viable policy objective. How, therefore, can this be achieved?

Formalizing the informal economy: direct and indirect policy measures

Reviewing the different policy measures for tackling the informal economy, two contrasting sets of measures are often differentiated. These have been variously labelled: "economic deterrence" versus "fiscal psychology" measures (Hasseldine & Li 1999); "chauvinistic" versus "softy" measures (Cullis & Lewis 1997); a "deterrence model" versus an "accommodative model" (Murphy 2005, 2008); "regulatory formalism" versus "responsive regulation" (Braithwaite 2002); "market-based" versus "rights-based" measures (Vainio 2012); "deterrence" versus "tax morale" measures (Ahmed & Braithwaite

2005); "command and control" versus "responsive regulation" measures (Commonwealth Association of Tax Administrators 2006); "sticks" versus "carrots" (Small Business Council 2004); or "deterrence" versus "enabling" measures (Williams 2004b, 2004c, 2006a).

These various labels are differentiating between "direct" compliance measures that punish non-compliant behaviour (and other less common approaches, including "direct" compliance measures that reward compliant behaviour), and "indirect" measures that tackle the formal institutional failures that lead to an incongruence between the norms, values and beliefs regarding whether it is acceptable to participate in the informal economy, and the formal rules of the game.

Table 5.1 summarizes the range of direct and indirect policy measures available to tackle the informal economy. The direct measures are grounded

Table 5.1 Policy approaches towards the informal economy

Approach	Tools	Examples of policy measures
Direct approach: deterrents	Improved detection	Data matching and sharing Joined up strategy Joint operations
	Increased penalties	Increased sanctions
	Increase perception of risk	Advertise penalties Advertise effectiveness of detection procedures
Direct approach: incentives	For employers	Simplification of compliance Direct and indirect tax incentives Support and advice
	For workers	Supply-side incentives (e.g. society-wide amnesties; voluntary disclosure; smoothing transition to formalization)
	For customers	Demand-side incentives (e.g. targeted direct and indirect taxes)
Indirect approach	Change employers, workers and customers attitudes (informal institutions)	Tax education Normative appeals Awareness raising of benefits of formality and costs of informality
	Change state (formal institutions)	Procedural and redistributive fairness and justice Wider economic and social developments

in the assumption that informal workers, businesses and consumers are rational economic actors. They therefore seek to ensure that the benefits of working in the informal economy are outweighed by the benefits of operating in the formal economy. This is accomplished using deterrence measures that increase the costs of non-compliance ("sticks") and/or by making the conduct of work in the formal economy more beneficial and easier ("carrots"). The indirect measures meanwhile, focus upon nurturing the "social contract" between the state and its citizens by fostering a high trust, high commitment culture and therefore self-regulation. Here, each set of measures is reviewed in turn.

Direct policy measures

Direct policy measures assume that participants in the informal economy are rational economic actors and as such, seek to alter the costs of engaging in the informal economy and benefits of operating formally. As the OECD (2008: 82) state, "Combating informal employment requires a comprehensive approach to reduce the costs and increase the benefits to business and workers of operating formally". First, therefore, the direct measures that seek to increase the costs of operating informally by detecting and punishing non-compliant behaviour are reviewed followed second, by the incentives that seek to increase the benefits of operating formally.

Deterrence measures: detecting and punishing participation in the informal economy

The use of deterrents to change behaviour has its origins in the classic utilitarian theory of crime of Jeremy Bentham (Bentham 1788) and Cesare Beccaria (Beccaria 1797), which sees citizens as rational actors who seek to maximize their expected utility. They weigh up the benefits and risks of an action and disobey the law if the expected penalty and probability of being caught is small relative to the benefits of disobeying the law.

This rational actor approach was popularized by Gary Becker (1968) in the late 1960s. He argued that governments must increase the costs of non-compliance so that compliant behaviour is a rational decision. By increasing the risks of detection and level of sanctions, criminal activity would become irrational behaviour. Prior to this, criminal behaviour was commonly viewed to result from mental illness and/or the social environment, with criminals depicted as victims of their circumstances.

In the early 1970s, Allingham and Sandmo (1972) applied this rational actor model to tax non-compliance and therefore, the informal economy. The non-compliant were depicted as making a rational economic decision because the benefits are greater than the expected cost of being caught and punished. Hence, they called for a change in the cost/benefit ratio confronting those engaged or thinking about participating in non-compliant behaviour. This rational economic actor approach was subsequently widely adopted (e.g. Grabiner 2000; Hasseldine & Li 1999; Job et al. 2007; Richardson & Sawyer 2001). It became commonplace for governments to seek to first, increase the perceived or actual likelihood of detection and/or second, increase the penalties for non-compliant behaviour.

When evaluating whether detecting and punishing non-compliance is an effective approach, however, it becomes quickly obvious that the evidence is far from conclusive. Some studies argue that increasing the probability of audit and detection reduces participation in the informal economy, at least for some income groups (Alm et al. 1995; Slemrod et al. 2001). Similarly, some studies argue that increasing fines reduces participation in the informal economy (Alm et al. 1995; De Juan et al. 1994; Feld & Frey 2002; Wenzel 2004).

However, a vast swathe of literature refutes the effectiveness of this deterrence approach (see Williams 2008a, 2008b). Many studies reveal that increasing penalties leads to either a growth in the informal economy, has no impact on its size, or only a short-term effect (Feld & Frey 2002; Murphy 2005). A similarly large body of evidence displays that increasing the probability of detection does not reduce the informal economy (e.g. Shaw et al. 2008). Instead, it leads to greater levels of non-compliance because of the breakdown of trust between the state and its citizens (Murphy & Harris 2007; Tyler et al. 2007). Indeed, the finding that many voluntarily comply even when the level of penalties and risks of detection compared with the benefits of being compliant warrant them acting in a non-compliant manner is perhaps the most telling criticism of the deterrence model and rational economic actor approach (Murphy 2008). If there is compliance even when it is not beneficial in rational economic actor terms, there must be other reasons beyond simply the risk of detection and level of punishment. The outcome is that many have begun to question the value of using deterrents alone. This is particularly the case when it is recognized that the objective is not simply to eradicate the informal economy, but rather, to transform informal work into formal work.

Incentives

If informal work is to be transformed into formal work, there has emerged a recognition that less emphasis is required on increasing the costs and risks of participation in informal work and that more emphasis needs to be put on increasing the benefits of formal work. The result is a widespread shift in approach across both supra-national institutions, such as the ILO and OECD (ILO 2015; OECD 2016), as well as across most national governments (Eurofound 2013; Williams & Nadin 2012a, 2013a, 2013b, 2014; Williams 2016, 2017a, 2017b), away from eradicating the informal economy, and towards formalizing the informal economy. This reflects an earlier literature advocating such an approach (Small Business Council 2004; Slemrod 1992; Williams 2006a).

So, detecting and punishing participation in the informal economy is replaced with rewarding compliant behaviour, rather than taking it as given. In other words, the emphasis is on rewarding "good" behaviour rather than punishing "bad" behaviour. When tackling the informal economy, this positive reinforcement approach based on the use of incentives (or what might be better viewed as "bribes") to change behaviour can take at least three forms (see Table 5.1): it can be made easier and/or more beneficial for businesses to participate in the formal economy; it can be made easier and/or more beneficial for individuals supplying informal work to engage in formal work; and it can be made easier and/or more beneficial for customers to use the formal rather than the informal economy to source goods and services.

For example, attempts have been made not only to increase the benefits of formality but also to simplify and reduce the costs of formalization (Woodruff *et al.* 2013). In a study of Kenya, Nick Devas and Roy Kelly (2001) report that a simplified "single business permit" for small firms was effective in encouraging formalization, as was a similar initiative in Uganda where reductions in the costs of formalization in Entebbe resulted in a 43 per cent increase in compliance (Sander 2003). In a study of Bolivia, Omar Garcia-Bolivar (2006) similarly reports that reducing the costs of formalization resulted in a 20 per cent increase in the number of firm registrations. However, a study of Lima in Peru (Jaramillo 2009) finds that only one in four firms that were offered free business licences and support with registration displayed a willingness to formalize, which is attributed to the recurrent costs of remaining formal along with the low perceived benefits of formalization, limited growth ambitions, and low trust in government. This therefore would suggest that reducing the costs of formality needs to be accompanied by initiatives to not only increase the benefits of operating in the formal economy but also to improve the social contract between government and citizens, employers and workers. Such a finding is reinforced by De Mel *et al.* (2012) who find that, in Sri Lanka, a financial offer equivalent to one-half to one month's median profits induced registration of about 20 per cent of firms, while a financial offer equivalent to two months' profits led to 50 per cent of firms registering. Greater attention, therefore, is being paid to identifying whether the perceived benefits of formalization are adequate and how to improve these benefits, rather than simply focusing upon reducing the costs of formalization or increasing the risks and costs of participation in the informal economy. Remaining central in this incentives approach however, is the belief that employers, workers and citizens are rational economic actors who weigh up the opportunities and risks of participation in the informal economy against the benefits of engagement in the formal economy.

Indirect policy measures

The problem with using direct policy measures to change behaviour is that individuals are not always rational economic actors and are not always in possession of perfect information. They have a limited ability to weigh up the costs and benefits, misperceive or do not perceive the true costs of their activities, and their actions are shaped by their social context. Perhaps most important, employers, workers and consumers are motivated not simply by self-interest in terms of what is most profitable for them but also by other motives, such as social customs, norms and morality but also a desire for redistribution and fairness (Alm 2011). Put another way, they are not simply profit-maximizing rational economic actors. Employers, workers and consumers are also social actors.

In recognizing this, there has been a shift away from solely using "sticks" and "carrots" to change behaviour and instead a greater focus upon improving the social contract between the state and employers, workers and consumers by pursuing the development of a high trust, high commitment culture (Alm *et al.* 1995; Andreoni *et al.* 1998; Torgler 2003; Weigel *et al.* 1987; Wenzel 2002). The objective in doing this is to encourage *voluntary* commitment to legitimate behaviour, rather than try to force employers, workers and consumers to comply using punishments and/or bribes. The use of such indirect policy measures to engender a social commitment to be compliant has a long history. More than a century ago, the German legal scholar, Georg von Schanz (1890) highlighted the key role of a tax contract between the state and its citizens. Some six decades later, moreover, the German "Cologne school of tax psychology" undertook a series of surveys to measure tax morale among taxpayers (see Schmölders 1952, 1960, 1962; Strümpel 1969), viewing it as an important and integral attitude that was strongly related to tax non-compliance (see Schmölders 1960). Although such research went into abeyance with the rise of the rational economic actor model in the 1970s, in recent years it has resurfaced as a policy approach (see e.g. Ketchen *et al.* 2014; Kirchler 1997, 1998, 1999, 2007; Torgler 2003, 2005a, 2005b, 2006a, 2006b, 2007, 2011).

In the contemporary period, this approach is grounded in institutional theory (North 1990). The underlying premise is that the informal economy arises when there is an asymmetry between the laws, codes and regulations of formal institutions and the norms, beliefs and values of informal institutions. When they are in symmetry, the informal economy does not exist, except unintentionally since the population will believe in conforming to the formal rules of the game. However, when the norms, values and beliefs differ to the laws and regulations, meaning that what formal institutions deem to be illegal activities are viewed as legitimate in terms of the norms, values and beliefs of the society or particular population groups, the informal economy prevails (Webb *et al.* 2009; Williams & Shahid 2016). To tackle the informal economy therefore, institutional asymmetry needs to be reduced. There are two strategies that can be used.

On the one hand, policy measures can be used to alter the norms, values and beliefs of the population (informal institutions) regarding the acceptability of the informal economy so that employers, workers and consumers' attitudes align with the formal rules of the game. On the other hand, policy measures can be used to alter the formal institutions so that they align better with the norms, values and beliefs of the wider society. In doing so, formal and informal institutions can become better aligned, resulting in a reduction in the informal economy due to greater voluntary compliance brought about by an intrinsic social commitment to operating in the formal economy. This approach thus seeks to achieve among the population what Benno Torgler (2003: 5) calls an "intrinsic motivation to pay taxes". Here employers, workers and consumers are viewed not as rational economic actors but rather, as social actors, and their cooperation is sought rather than pursue attempts to coerce them to comply.

On the other hand, changes in formal institutions can be pursued to achieve this alignment between the formal and informal institutions. These are of two kinds. First, changes can be sought in the processes of formal institutions in terms of fairness, procedural justice and redistributive justice. Fairness refers to the extent to which employers and workers believe they are paying their fair share compared with others (Wenzel 2004; Murphy et al. 2009). Redistributive justice refers to whether they receive the goods and services they believe that they deserve given the taxes that they pay (Richardson & Sawyer 2001) and procedural justice to the degree to which they believe that governments treat them in an impartial, respectful and responsible manner (Braithwaite & Reinhart 2000; Murphy 2005).

Secondly, changes in the products of formal institutions can be sought in the form of wider economic and social developments in recognition that the informal economy is in large part a by-product of broader economic and social conditions. Until now, and as Chapter 2 showed, there have been four contrasting theoretical standpoints regarding what broader economic and social policies might encourage formalization, namely the modernization, neoliberal and political economy theses and institutional theory. Chapter 3 showed that formal institutional failures identified by modernization and political economy theory (e.g. low levels of economic development, a lack of modernization of governance, too little state intervention in work and welfare) result in institutional asymmetry and thus the greater prevalence of the informal economy.

Combining direct and indirect policy measures

To tackle the informal economy, it is not a choice between using either direct or indirect policy measures. Although the focus of most national governments until recently when seeking eradication has been upon direct

measures, especially deterrence measures that increase the costs of participating in the informal economy by increasing the risks of detection and
levels of punishment (see ILO 2015; OECD 2016; Williams 2015d), this
does not mean that the solution is therefore to use either "incentives" or
indirect measures as a replacement when seeking to formalize the informal
economy. Direct and indirect policy measures are not mutually exclusive
(Eurofound 2013; Williams 2014a, 2017a, 2017b).

Indeed, supra-national institutions have recognized that this is the
case and that it is necessary to use *both* direct and indirect policy measures. Following the adoption of Recommendation 204, which recognized
that the aim in tackling the informal economy is to formalize the informal
economy, the ILO (2017) have adopted a "strategic compliance" approach,
which recognizes the need for compliance authorities to adopt both direct
and indirect measures when tackling the informal economy. Similarly, the
European Commission's European Platform Tackling Undeclared Work has
adopted a "holistic approach". This is where a whole government approach
is adopted, joining-up at the level of both strategy and operations the policy
fields of labour, tax and social security law, and which uses the full range of
direct and *indirect* policy measures available to enhance the power of, and
trust in, authorities respectively (Williams 2017b).

How, therefore, might this operate in practice? An example is that governments may target key country-level macroeconomic and social conditions that have a direct influence on the prevalence of the informal economy,
change the organizational culture of government departments, such as
tax offices and labour inspectorates, towards a more customer-oriented
approach, and introduce public campaigns to encourage a commitment to
compliance, whilst simplifying regulatory compliance for business start-ups
and introducing incentives for employers, workers and customers to operate
in the formal economy (e.g. amnesties, tax deductions). However, and at the
same time, and in relation to those who fail to comply, sanctions might be
used along with improvements in the ability to detect those operating in the
informal economy.

In consequence, the debate is not whether to use either direct or indirect
policy measures. The emergent consensus in policy circles is that both are
required. Instead, the major issue is determining which specific policy measures in each approach are most effective and what is the most effective way
of putting these measures together in various combinations and sequences

to engender compliance in an effective manner. For example, measures to improve detection through inspections are currently often combined with campaigns to raise awareness. Tougher sanctions furthermore, often follow amnesties and voluntary disclosure schemes. However, whether these are the most effective combinations and sequences to formalize the informal economy needs to be evaluated. Nevertheless, two approaches have emerged in the scholarly literature that offer different ways of combining and sequencing these direct and indirect policy measures, namely the responsive regulation approach and the slippery slope framework.

Responsive regulation

Responsive regulation engages employers, workers and consumers to take responsibility for operating in a manner consistent with the formal rules of the game. This approach pursues measures to win their "hearts and minds" to elicit a culture of commitment to the formal rules. In doing so, the need for external rules to regulate employers, workers and consumers is avoided. However, even if this approach gives primacy to the use of indirect policy measures, it is not exclusively limited to such measures (see Braithwaite 2009).

The Australian Tax Office, for example, is one such enforcement authority that has moved towards adopting this responsive regulation approach. In the first instance indirect measures are used to elicit voluntary adherence to the formal rules. This is then followed by persuasion using incentives and encouragement, and only as a last resort for the small minority still refusing to comply with the formal rules are deterrence measures used (Braithwaite 2009; Job *et al.* 2007). In other words, the responsive regulation approach is based on a regulatory pyramid. The underpinning belief is that in most cases a compliance authority will not need to employ deterrents to achieve adherence to the formal rules. Instead, it can start with indirect policy measures, and only if these do not produce adherence to the formal rules with some groups, then are direct incentives used on these groups, with deterrents only used as a last resort. The level of intervention therefore escalates up the pyramid until it reaches the policy intervention that elicits adherence.

The recognition is that there exists a continuum of attitudes towards being compliant, and that different policy measures are appropriate for each different motivational posture. The outcome is that policy measures are temporally sequenced, starting with indirect policy measures which are applied to the majority of employers, workers and consumers who adopt a positive motivational posture (i.e. commitment to being compliant), and feel morally committed to follow the formal rules, then direct incentives for those with less positive motivational postures (i.e. capitulation, resistance), and only after these fail are direct deterrence measures employed for those disengaged from the formal institutions and adopting a very negative motivational posture (Braithwaite 2003).

However, whether this is the appropriate temporal sequence is open to question. Until now, there have been no evaluations of whether this sequencing is the most appropriate or effective way of eliciting commitment to the formal rules of the game. Although it might appear logically to be the appropriate and even most effective way of eliciting compliance, there is no current evidence-base that this is the case.

Slippery slope framework

Another way of combining direct and indirect policy measures is to adopt the "slippery slope framework" (Kirchler *et al.* 2008). This again distinguishes two types of compliance approach: voluntary compliance (achieved using indirect policy measures) and enforced compliance (achieved using direct policy measures). Voluntary compliance is viewed as occurring where there is trust in the authorities. Enforced compliance, meanwhile, is viewed as requiring the authorities to have power (i.e. the ability to get citizens to do what they were before not going to do, in the way in which the authorities wish them to do it). When there is neither trust in authorities and authorities have no power, then authorities find themselves on a slippery slope and the informal economy will be more prevalent.

To formalize the informal economy therefore, governments can either increase the power of authorities and/or trust in the authorities. Direct policy measures, as shown above, are used to increase the power of authorities, whilst the indirect measures are used to increase trust in authorities. In this approach, however, it is recommended that both are used concurrently to formalize the informal economy. The slippery slope framework therefore seeks to use both at the same time to achieve the formalization of the informal economy.

In recent years, there has started to emerge an evidence-base that this concurrent combining of voluntary and enforced compliance is the most effective approach. Kogler *et al.* (2013) undertake an experiment to manipulate the power of authorities and citizens' trust in authorities using scenario techniques, and to assess the intentions to declare taxes honestly in four European countries: Austria, Hungary, Romania and Russia. The intention is to test the impact of power and trust on compliance in countries with different institutional, political and societal characteristics. In a 2×2 design, scenarios described authorities as either trustworthy or untrustworthy, and as either powerful or powerless. The resultant finding is that intentions to declare taxes honestly were highest in all countries if the authorities were described as powerful and trustworthy. Evasion was high if both power and trust were at a minimum. In addition, perceptions of high power boosted enforced compliance, whereas high trust was related to strong voluntary cooperation.

In a further study, based on a survey of 476 self-employed, Kogler *et al.* (2015) show that perceptions of procedural and distributive justice predict voluntary compliance, and trust in authorities mediates this relationship. In addition, the relationship between retributive justice (i.e. the perceived fairness with regard to the sanctioning of self-employed tax evaders) and enforced compliance is mediated by power, which is the perceived deterrence of authorities' enforcement strategies. With regard to both retributive justice and deterrence, a mediational effect of trust on the relation to voluntary compliance was identified. Moreover, voluntary and enforced compliance were related to perceived social norms, but these relations were mediated neither by trust nor power.

In a further extension of the slippery slope framework, Gangl *et al.* (2012) distinguish three climates: a service climate, an antagonistic climate and a confidence climate. They argue that a service climate requires the legitimate power of authorities and that this leads to reason-based trust on the part of citizens and increases voluntary compliance. An antagonistic climate meanwhile, occurs when the coercive power of authorities prevails, leading to enforced compliance and an atmosphere where authorities and citizens work against each other. A confidence climate, finally, is characterized by an implicit trust between authorities and citizens (an unintentional and automatic form of trust) which results in the perception of compliance as a moral obligation and again the voluntary cooperation of citizens.

That power and trust are essential for good governance is also now being seriously considered by authorities in various countries (OECD 2013). For instance, in order to improve interactions with their clientele, tax administrators in the Netherlands and Austria have started pilot projects for young entrepreneurs. Duties and service facilities are explained to these inexperienced taxpayers, and cooperation, rather than control, is fostered right from the start of a business. In the "fair-play" initiative, Austrian tax authorities emphasize differences between taxpayers in their willingness to pay and the importance of reacting with adequate regulation strategies ranging from deterrence to support (Müller 2012). In 2005, moreover, the Dutch Tax and Customs Administration introduced a pioneering supervisory approach, "horizontal monitoring", as an alternative to the traditional "vertical monitoring". This approach is based on the firm conviction that a positive relationship, based on mutual trust, between taxpayers, tax practitioners, and tax authorities, reduces unnecessary supervisory costs and burdens, complex discussions about tax designs on the edge of legality, and aggressive tax planning with retrospective adjustments (Committee Horizontal Monitoring Tax and Customs Administration 2012). More widely, the European Commission's Platform Tackling Undeclared Work has argued that the way to implement the "holistic approach" is through using a "full policy operationalisation model". This model combines the direct and indirect policy measures concurrently, based on the above evidence that a high trust, high power approach is the most effective in tackling the informal economy.

In sum, the argument of the slippery slope approach is that employers, workers and citizens follow the formal rules of the game either because they fear detection and fines due to the power of authorities (enforced compliance) or because they feel a commitment to be honest because they have trust in the authorities (voluntary cooperation). When there is effective enforced compliance as well as high voluntary cooperation (i.e. both power and trust), the informal economy is less prevalent. When there is ineffective enforced compliance and little voluntary cooperation, the informal economy is more extensive.

Conclusions

This chapter has reviewed how the informal economy can be tackled. To commence, it has examined four policy goals, namely taking no action, eradicating the informal economy, deregulating the formal economy, and formalizing the informal economy. This has shown that doing nothing leaves intact the current negative consequences of the informal economy for formal businesses and workers (e.g. unfair competition), informal enterprises and workers (e.g. the inability to gain access to credit to expand), consumers (e.g. no guarantee of health and safety standards) and governments and the wider society and economy (e.g. taxes owed are not collected). Eradicating the informal economy would result in governments deterring precisely the entrepreneurship and active citizenship that they otherwise wish to foster, whilst deregulating the formal economy would level down rather than level up working conditions. Formalizing the informal economy is thus revealed as the most viable approach. This is also the consensus view of supra-national institutions operating in this policy realm (European Commission 2016; ILO 2015; Williams 2017). How, therefore, can this be achieved?

This chapter has outlined that this can be accomplished using either direct and/or indirect policy measures, and the range of direct measures have been outlined along with the various indirect policy measures that can be used. This has shown that the currently dominant approach of using direct deterrence measures that improve the probability of detection and increase the punishment for participation in the informal economy is a limited approach and that there is a much more comprehensive range of tools available for formalizing the informal economy. These various tools, moreover, are not mutually exclusive.

To demonstrate this, the final section of this chapter has reviewed various policy approaches that can be adopted which combine direct and indirect policy measures when seeking to formalize the informal economy, namely a responsive regulation approach and a slippery slope framework. The various policy choices, approaches and measures available to policy makers have been outlined, along with suggestions regarding how they can be combined and sequenced. The conclusion has been that both direct policy measures are required to increase the power of authorities as well as indirect policy measures to increase trust in authorities.

6

Conclusions and future directions

Introduction

The aim of this concluding chapter is to synthesize the material from the previous chapters and to draw conclusions about the way forward for measuring, explaining and tackling the informal economy. To do so, the starting point is the set of questions posed at the start of this book. What different theories have been used to explain the informal economy and how have the dominant theoretical explanations changed over time? How can the informal economy be measured and what is its size? What types of informal work exist, who does it and what are their motives for participating in the informal economy? And what policy options are available for tackling the informal economy? What is the current approach being pursued and why, and what alternative policy approaches and measures might be instead used to tackle the informal economy? In this concluding chapter, how these questions have been answered will be reviewed along with fruitful future directions for research on the informal economy.

Defining the informal economy

Reviewing the competing enterprise-, jobs- and activity-based definitions, the informal economy was defined in Chapter 1 as *socially legitimate paid work that is not declared to, hidden from, or unregistered with, the authorities for tax, social security and/or labour law purposes when it should be declared.* If the activity is illegal in other respects and/or deemed socially illegitimate, then this activity is not considered part of the informal economy but instead part of the criminal economy (e.g. forced labour, selling stolen goods, trafficking illegal drugs) which is both illegal from the viewpoint of formal institutions and illegitimate from the viewpoint of informal institutions. Given the strong consensus amongst scholars about what is the informal economy, and what is not, there is seen to be little need for future research to expend much energy on defining the informal economy.

The only issue that might be considered in this regard is that the above definition of the informal economy adopted in this book gives a little too much emphasis to agency when defining the informal economy. It perhaps implicitly, albeit unintentionally, intimates that engaging in the informal economy is a choice. It does not make explicit who is not declaring it, hiding it or not registering it. For this reason, it is perhaps the case that scholars need to make it explicit who is deciding not to declare, hide or register such activity when they report their studies.

Reviewing the consequences of the existence of the informal economy, it was shown that it has different consequences for different stakeholders, namely formal enterprises, informal businesses, informal workers, customers of the informal economy, governments, and the wider economy and society. Examining these consequences, it was revealed that the informal economy is important to study not for one individual reason but for many reasons. For all the above stakeholders, the finding is that the negative consequences appear to markedly outweigh any positive consequences. However, the important finding is that there have been few, if any, studies that have sought to calculate the actual impacts of the informal economy.

Future research, therefore, could usefully seek to develop a more evidence-based approach to the positive and negative impacts of the informal economy on each of the different stakeholder groups. For example, studies could be conducted of the extent to which the development of enterprises operating in the informal economy are constrained by their inability to: gain access to finance capital; advertise their business openly to attract new customers; secure the formal intellectual property rights to their process and product innovations, and access business support and advice. Similarly, studies could measure the degree to which informal workers: do not have standard employment rights (e.g. annual and other leave, sickness and redundancy pay, and training); lack other legal rights (e.g. minimum wage, maximum working hours); are affected by the inability to build-up rights to the state pension and other contributory benefits, and access occupational pension schemes; lack access to health and safety standards in the workplace; have lower job security compared with formal employees; lose employability due to their lack of evidence of prior engagement in employment; are unable to gain access to credit (e.g. mortgages or loans) since they have no evidence of their income; are unable to get an employer's reference; and suffer from a fear of detection.

Theorizing the informal economy

In Chapter 2, the different theories used to explain the informal economy were reviewed along with how the dominant theoretical explanations have changed over time. This revealed that for most of the twentieth century, modernization theory was dominant. This viewed the informal economy as a residue from a pre-modern economic system and as disappearing with the modernization of economies and societies. As such, the informal economy is viewed as persisting only due to economic underdevelopment and a lack of modernization of governance.

However, the recognition over the past three decades that the informal economy is a continuously prevailing feature of contemporary economies, has led to the emergence of alternative explanations. On the one hand, a political economy perspective has emerged which views the informal economy as an inherent feature of contemporary capitalism which is growing as firms outsource and sub-contract production to informal workers and enterprises, and workers are pushed into the informal economy as a coping strategy in the absence of other means of survival. Here, therefore, the informal economy persists due to inadequate state intervention in work and welfare, and a lack of protection of workers. On the other hand, and conversely, a neoliberal perspective has depicted the informal economy to result from over-regulation of the economy, such as high taxes and burdensome regulations and controls, and thus views workers and businesses as voluntarily exiting the formal economy.

None of these theories, nevertheless, each of which focus upon various national-level structural determinants, has been able to explain why some workers and businesses in a country turn to the informal economy and others do not. Chapter 2 thus concluded by examining how institutional theory has been used to explain why some workers and businesses engage in the informal economy and others do not. From this institutionalist perspective, all societies have both formal institutions (i.e. codified laws and regulations) that set out the legal rules of the game, as well as informal institutions which are the unwritten socially shared rules expressed in the norms, values and beliefs of employers, workers and citizens (Helmke & Levitsky 2004). Work in the informal economy takes place outside of the formal institutional prescriptions but within the norms, values and beliefs of informal institutions (Godfrey 2011; Kistruck *et al.* 2015; Siqueira *et al.* 2016; Webb *et al.* 2009; Welter *et al.* 2015). In first-wave institutional theory, the informal economy was explained as resulting from formal institutional failings, as described above in modernization, neoliberal and/or political economy. However, in a second wave of institutional theory, it was recognized that focusing upon solely formal institutional failings ignores the role played by informal institutions (Godfrey 2015; North 1990; Scott 2008) and the informal economy was seen to arise due to the asymmetry between formal and informal institutions (Webb *et al.* 2009). In this book, a third wave of institutional thought has been introduced. This has synthesized the two previous waves by arguing that when formal institutional failures result in an asymmetry between formal and informal institutions, the result is bigger informal economies.

Future research could now focus upon evaluating this third wave of institutional theory. To do so, what is required is to evaluate not only whether there is a significant relationship between the extent of the informal economy and the degree of vertical trust (i.e. the trust of employers, workers and citizens in the formal institutions), but also which precise formal institutional failings lead to this lack of vertical trust (e.g. public sector corruption, low social expenditure, lack of intervention in the labour market to protect vulnerable groups, types of formal institutional instability and uncertainty). Without doubt, this will require studies of whether the cross-national variations in the size of the informal economy are associated with the degree of vertical trust and such formal institutional failings.

Measuring the size of the informal economy

To show how this might be undertaken, Chapter 3 reviewed the various direct and indirect measurement methods used to estimate the size of the informal economy and provided various estimates of how the size of the informal economy varies between countries using both indirect measurement methods and direct surveys. It also started to evaluate the validity of the various theoretical explanations for the prevalence of the informal economy by analysing whether cross-national variations in the size of the informal economy (using both direct and indirect methods) are correlated with economic underdevelopment and a lack of modernization of governance (modernization theory), too little state intervention in work and welfare (political economy theory), state over-interference in the form of high taxes and over-burdensome regulations (neoliberal theory) and the relevance of institutional theory.

The first study reported the results of an indirect measurement method that estimated the varying size of the informal economy across the member states of the European Union by evaluating the discrepancy between reported labour inputs from the supply-side (namely, labour force surveys) and reported labour inputs from the demand-side (namely business surveys). Based on the assumption that enterprises may try to hide labour inputs in the informal economy, the discrepancy is a measure of the informal economy. Using this labour input method (LIM), the finding was that 9.3 per cent of total labour input in the private sector in the European Union is in the informal economy, and that the informal economy constitutes 14.3 per cent of GVA in the private sector. However, marked variations in the size of the informal economy across countries were identified, ranging from 25 per cent of total GVA in Poland, Romania and Lithuania, to 7 per cent in Germany. Evaluating the different theoretical explanations, the finding was that the size of the informal economy is higher where there is institutional asymmetry, and that the formal institutional failures strongly associated with larger informal economies are weak GDP per capita, a lack of modernization of government and higher levels of corruption, state under-intervention in work and welfare, and greater inequality.

The second study reports the results of a direct survey of 36 developing countries. This again reveals that across all these developing countries, three out of every five (59.8%) non-agricultural workers have their main employment in the informal economy. This is an important finding. Most workers in developing countries have their main employment in the informal economy. It is the informal economy, therefore, not the formal economy, that employs most of the workers in the developing world. However, marked variations again exist in the proportion employed in the informal economy across countries, ranging from 84.7 per cent of the non-agricultural workforce in Mali to 6.5 per cent in Serbia. Evaluating the contrasting theoretical explanations, it is again revealed that institutional asymmetry is strongly correlated with the size of the informal economy, and that the formal institutional failures across the developing world that are significantly associated with larger informal economies are again those proposed by modernization and political economy theory.

In future, nevertheless, more research will be required on this issue. Not only are more cross-national data sets required that survey the size of the informal economy across countries using harmonized data and methods, but there is also a need for regression analyses that analyse whether the structural conditions associated with larger informal economies remain significant when other variables are included and held constant. It is not only the size of the informal economy, however, that is important to understand. So too is there a need for greater understanding of the characteristics of the informal economy.

Characteristics of the informal economy

Chapter 4 sought to understand the characteristics, rather than magnitude, of the informal economy. It reviewed the different varieties of work in the informal economy, who does it and why they do it. The finding was that: informal work ranges from types of informal waged employment through varieties of informal self-employment to paid favours; all social groups engage in informal work, although some are more likely to do so (e.g. younger age groups, those with financial difficulties), and that the motives for participating in the informal economy range from purely economic necessity through to purely voluntary choice. An outcome was the identification of the existence of a dual informal labour market composed of a lower tier of necessity-driven informal workers and an upper-tier of informal workers who engage in the informal economy more out of choice. The ratio of lower- to upper-tier informal workers, however, varies across not only geographical areas (e.g. affluent and deprived countries or localities) but also across socio-economic groups.

Until now, nevertheless, compared with studies that evaluate the magnitude of the informal economy, very little research has been conducted on the multifarious types of informal work, who works in the informal economy and why they do so. Much more future research is required on an individual country-level. Such research is important. Unless it is known who engages in informal work, what they do, and why they do it, then it will not be possible to develop targeted policies to tackle this sphere.

This is because different types of informal work conducted by various groups for different reasons require different policy responses. For example, if a significant proportion of informal work is conducted by the unemployed on a self-employed basis, then policies to smooth the transition from unemployment to self-employment will be necessary. However, if most informal work is conducted as waged work, then such a policy measure to smooth the transition from unemployment to self-employment will be irrelevant. Similarly, if most informal work is a voluntary choice due to corruption in the public sector, or a lack of belief in what government is seeking to achieve, it will be more relevant to pursue reform of the formal institutions in terms of developing redistributive and procedural justice and fairness, coupled with structural changes (e.g. the introduction of welfare "safety nets"), complemented by education and awareness-raising campaigns about the benefits of operating in the formal economy. In-depth research is therefore required in different contexts in the future on who engages in informal work, what they do, and why they do it, so that policies can be developed which are tailored to the character of the informal work and the type of informal worker that is most prevalent in each context.

Policy options and approaches

To understand what can be done to tackle the informal economy, Chapter 5 reviewed four hypothetical policy options, namely: taking no action; eradicating the informal economy; deregulating the formal economy; or transforming informal work into formal work. This revealed that doing nothing leaves intact the current negative consequences of the informal economy for formal businesses and workers (e.g. unfair competition), informal enterprises and workers (e.g. the inability to gain access to credit to expand), consumers (e.g. no guarantee of health and safety standards) and governments and the wider society and economy (e.g. taxes owed are not collected). Eradicating the informal economy would result in governments deterring precisely the entrepreneurship and active citizenship that they otherwise wish to foster, whilst deregulating the formal economy would level down rather than level up working conditions. Formalizing the informal economy is thus revealed as the most viable approach. This is also the consensus view of most national governments and supra-national institutions operating in this policy realm (European Commission 2016; ILO 2015; Williams 2017).

Given this goal of formalizing the informal economy, Chapter 5 then reviewed the policy measures available for achieving this objective. This set out two broad sets of policy measures. On the one hand, direct policy measures were outlined that not only seek to dissuade participation in the informal economy but also to incentivize and encourage participation in the formal economy. These direct policy measures therefore seek to directly increase the costs and reduce the benefits of informality, and to reduce the costs and increase the benefits of participating in the formal economy. In doing so, the intention is to address those formal institutional failures, such as the powerlessness of formal institutions, which result in the greater prevalence of the informal economy. Using direct policy measures alone, nevertheless, does not solve the full range of formal institutional failures that result in institutional asymmetry and therefore bigger informal economies. Direct policy measures address only one formal institutional failing that produces bigger informal economies, namely the relative powerlessness of the enforcement regime.

On the other hand, therefore, and to address the other formal institutional failures that result in institutional symmetry and the greater prevalence of the informal economy, indirect policy measures were outlined. These measures address the other formal institutional failings, namely formal institutional resource misallocations and inefficiencies, voids and weaknesses, and the instability and uncertainty of formal institutions. Indirect policy measures are of two kinds. First, and to reduce institutional asymmetry, there are educational and awareness-raising initiatives that seek to align the norms, values and beliefs of employers, workers and citizens with the formal rules of the game (i.e. laws and regulations). However, the likelihood that such campaigns can align the formal and informal institutions is small, unless the other formal institutional failures are resolved that produce this institutional asymmetry, namely the formal institutional resource misallocations and inefficiencies, and the formal institutional voids and weaknesses.

Secondly, therefore, reform of the formal institutions is required to make them more palatable to employers, workers and citizens. The policy initiatives required to achieve this include not only a variety of process innovations across government that develop the perceived level of procedural and redistributive justice and fairness of government, so as to improve institutional symmetry, but also changes in the economic and social conditions which are significantly associated with greater institutional asymmetry, such as improving social expenditure, labour market interventions to protect vulnerable groups, and the level of inequality and deprivation in societies.

Direct and indirect policy measures, however, were revealed not to be either/or choices. They are not mutually exclusive. Given that each set of measures addresses a different set of formal institutional failures, both are required to tackle the informal economy. The debate in recent years about how these should be combined and sequenced was reviewed. This revealed how on the one hand, a responsive regulation approach has been advocated which combines all these approaches but sequences them by starting with the indirect policy measures and if these do not have the desired effect, then direct incentives are used to encourage formalization and as a last resort when all else fails, direct deterrents are employed (Braithwaite 2002). And on the other hand, how a slippery slope approach has been advocated, which argues that compliance is greatest when both the power of authorities (achieved using direct policy measures) and trust in authorities (achieved using indirect policy measures) is high (Kirchler *et al.* 2008). If either the power of, or trust in, authorities is low, then governments will find themselves on a slippery slope and the result will be larger informal economies.

Which way of combining and sequencing direct and indirect policy measures is most effective in different contexts requires evaluation. To obtain a fuller understanding of how to combine and sequence the direct and indirect policy measures, will require more evidence-based evaluations of which individual policy measures work and which do not, albeit perhaps in conjunction with other measures, in individual contexts. Currently, few evaluations exist of the effectiveness of individual policy measures, never mind their effectiveness when used in conjunction with other measures, or in which contexts. There is therefore a considerable amount of research required before solutions for specific contexts can be firmly advocated.

Hopefully, nevertheless, this book has started to detail the range of policy measures required to formalize the informal economy. This has revealed that direct deterrence policy measures alone, which increase the penalties and risks of detection, are not going to result in a formalization of the informal economy. The shift away from eradicating the informal economy and to formalizing the informal economy as the policy goal, necessitates that governments adopt a much wider range of policy measures.

In sum, if this book results in less normative portrayals of the informal economy and more evidence-based evaluations of the extent and characteristics of work in the informal economy and its various consequences in different contexts, then it will have fulfilled one of its major intentions. If the outcome is more considered evidence-based decisions on what should be done about the informal economy, along with a shift away from simply seeking to eradicate it by increasing the penalties and risks of detection, and towards using the full range of direct and indirect policy measures, then this book will have achieved its wider intention.

References

Acemoglu, D. & J. Robinson 2012. *Why Nations Fail: The Origins of Power, Prosperity and Poverty*. London: Profile.

Adom, K. & C. Williams 2012a. "Evaluating the explanations for the informal economy in third world cities: some evidence from Koforidua in the eastern region of Ghana". *International Entrepreneurship and Management Journal* 8(3), 309–24.

Adom, K. & C. Williams 2012b. "Evaluating the motives of informal entrepreneurs in Koforidua, Ghana". *Journal of Developmental Entrepreneurship* 17(1), 1–21.

Adom, K. & C. Williams 2014. "Evaluating the explanations for the informal economy in third world cities: some evidence from Koforidua in the eastern region of Ghana". *International Entrepreneurship and Management Journal* 10(2), 427–45.

Ahmed, E. & Y. Braithwaite 2005. "Understanding small business taxpayers: issues of deterrence, tax morale, fairness and work practice". *International Small Business Journal* 23(5), 539–68.

Aidis, R. & M. Van Praag 2007. "Illegal entrepreneurship experience: does it make a difference for business performance and motivation?". *Journal of Business Venturing* 22(2), 283–310.

Aliyev, H. 2015. "Post-Soviet informality: towards theory-building". *International Journal of Sociology and Social Policy* 35(3/4), 182–98.

Allingham, M. & A. Sandmo 1972. "Income tax evasion: a theoretical analysis". *Journal of Public Economics* 1(2), 323–38.

Alm, J. 2011. "Designing alternative strategies to reduce tax evasion". In M. Pickhardt & A. Prinz (eds), *Tax Evasion and the Shadow Economy*, 13–32. Cheltenham: Elgar.

Alm, J., E. Martinez-Vazque & B. Torgler 2006. "Russian attitudes toward paying taxes: before, during and after the transition". *International Journal of Social Economics* 33(12), 832–57.

Alm, J., I. Sanchez & A. De Juan 1995. "Economic and non-economic factors in tax compliance". *Kyklos* 48, 3–18.

Alm, J. & B. Torgler 2006. "Culture differences and tax morale in the United States and in Europe". *Journal of Economic Psychology* 27(2), 224–46.

Andreoni, J., B. Erard & J. Fainstein 1998. "Tax compliance". *Journal of Economic Literature* 36(2), 818–60.

Andrews, D., A. Caldera Sanchez & A. Johansson 2011. *Towards a Better Understanding of the Informal Economy*. Paris: OECD Economics Department.

Apel, M. 1994. "An expenditure-based estimate of tax evasion in Sweden". Stockholm: RSV Tax Reform Evaluation Report No.1.

Autio, E. & K. Fu 2015. "Economic and political institutions and entry into formal and informal entrepreneurship". *Asia Pacific Journal of Management* 32(1), 67–94.

Bàculo, L. 2001. The shadow economy in Italy: results from field studies. Paper presented at the European Scientific Workshop on *The shadow economy: empirical evidence and new policy issues at the European level*, Ragusa, Sicily, September 20–21.

Bajada, C. 2002. *Australia's Cash Economy: A Troubling Issue for Policymakers*. Aldershot: Ashgate.

Bajada, C. & F. Schneider 2005. "Introduction". In C. Bajada & F. Schneider (eds), *Size, Causes and Consequences of the Underground Economy: An International Perspective*, 1–14. Aldershot: Ashgate.

Barbour, A. & M. Llanes 2013. *Supporting People to Legitimise their Informal Businesses*. York: Rowntree Foundation.

Bardhan, P. 1997. "Corruption and development: a review of issues". *Journal of Economic Literature* 35, 1320–46.

Barone, G. & S. Mocetti 2009. "Tax morale and public spending in efficiency". Economic Working Paper no. 732, Rome: Bank of Italy.

Barsoum, G. 2015. "Striving for job security: the lived experience of employment informality among educated youth in Egypt". *International Journal of Sociology and Social Policy* 35(5/6), 340–58.

Bartlett, B. 1998. "The underground economy". National Center for Policy Analysis. Available at: http://www.ncpa.org/ba/ba273.html (accessed 12 June 2018).

Baumol, W. & A. Blinder 2008. *Macroeconomics: Principles and Policy*. Cincinnati, OH: South-Western Publishing.

Beccaria, C. [1797] (1986). *On Crimes and Punishment*. Indianapolis, IN: Hackett.

Becker, G. 1968. "Crime and punishment: an econometric approach". *Journal of Political Economy* 76(1), 169–217.

Becker, K. 2004. *The Informal Economy*. Stockholm: Swedish International Development Agency.

Bentham, J. [1788] (1983). "Principles of penal law". In J. Burton (ed.), *The Works of Jeremy Bentham*, 42–61. Philadelphia: Lea & Blanchard.

Bergman, M. & N. Nevarez 2006. "Do audits enhance compliance? An empirical assessment of VAT enforcement". *National Tax Journal* 59(4), 817–32.

Bhattacharya, S. 2014. "Is labour still a relevant category for praxis? Critical reflections on some contemporary discourses on work and labour in capitalism". *Development and Change* 45(5), 941–62.

Bhowmik, S. 2005. "Street vendors in Asia: a review". *Economic and Political Weekly*, 28 May–4 June, 2256–64.

Bird, R., J. Martinez-Vazquez & B. Torgler 2006. "Societal institutions and tax effort in developing countries". In J. Alm, J. Martinez-Vazquez & M. Rider (eds), *The Challenges of Tax Reform in the Global Economy*, 286–338. New York: Springer.

Boeke, J. 1942. *Economies and Economic Policy in Dual Societies*. Harlem: Tjeenk Willnik.

Boels, D. 2014. "It's better than stealing: informal street selling in Brussels". *International Journal of Sociology and Social Policy* 34(9/10), 670–93.

Braithwaite, J. 2002. *Restorative Justice and Responsive Regulation*. New York: Oxford University Press.

Braithwaite, V. 2003. "Dancing with tax authorities: motivational postures and non-compliant actions". In V. Braithwaite (ed.), *Taxing Democracy*, 1–11. Aldershot: Ashgate.

Braithwaite V. 2009. *Defiance in Taxation and Governance: Resisting and Dismissing Authority in a Democracy*. Cheltenham: Elgar.

Braithwaite, V. & M. Reinhart 2000. "The taxpayers' charter: does the Australian tax office comply and who benefits?". Centre for Tax System Integrity Working Paper no.1. Canberra: Australian National University.

Brill, L. 2010. *Understanding Women's Experience of Working in the Informal Economy in Salford*. Manchester: Oxfam.

Brill, L. 2011. *Women's Participation in the Informal Economy: What Can We Learn From Oxfam's Work?* Manchester: Oxfam.

Bromley, R. 2007. "Foreword". In J. Cross & A. Morales (eds), *Street Entrepreneurs: People, Place and Politics in Local and Global Perspective*, 1–12. London: Routledge.

Browne, K. 2004. *Creole Economics: Caribbean Cunning Under the French Flag*. Austin, TX: University of Texas Press.

Button, K. 1984. "Regional variations in the irregular economy: a study of possible trends". *Regional Studies* 18(3), 385–92.

Caridi, P. & P. Passerini 2001. "The underground economy, the demand for currency approach and the analysis of discrepancies: some recent European experience". *Review of Income and Wealth* 47(2), 239–50.

Castells, M. & A. Portes 1989. "World underneath: the origins, dynamics and effects of the informal economy". In A. Portes, M. Castells & L. Benton (eds), *The Informal Economy: Studies in Advanced and Less Developing Countries*, 19–41. Baltimore, MD: John Hopkins University Press.

Cebula, R. 1997. "An empirical analysis of the impact of government tax and auditing policies on the size of the underground economy: the case of the United States, 1993–94". *American Journal of Economics and Sociology* 56(2), 173–85.

Charron, N., L. Dijkstra & V. Lapuente 2015. "Mapping the regional divide in Europe: a measure for assessing quality of government in 206 European regions". *Social Indicators Research* 122(2), 315–46.

Chatterjee, S., K. Chaudhury & F. Schneider 2002. "The size and development of the Indian shadow economy and a comparison with 18 Asian countries: an empirical investigation". University of Linz Department of Economics discussion paper.

Chen, C., Chen, X.-P. & S. Huang 2012. "Chinese guanxi: an integrative review and new directions for future research". *Management and Organization Review* 9(1), 167–207.

Chen, M. 2012. *The Informal Economy: Definitions, Theories and Policies*. Manchester: Women in Informal Employment Global and Organising.

Cocco, M. & E. Santos 1984. "A economia subterranea: contributos para a sua analisee quanticacao no caso Portugues". *Buletin Trimestral do Banco de Portugal* 6(1), 5–15.

Coletto, D. & L. Bisschop 2017. "Waste pickers in the informal economy of the global South: included or excluded?". *International Journal of Sociology and Social Policy*, 37(5/6), 280–94.

Committee Horizontal Monitoring Tax and Customs Administration 2012. *Tax Supervision – Made to Measure: Flexible when Possible, Strict where Necessary*. The Hague. Available at: http://www.ifa.nl/Document/Publicaties/Enhanced%20Relationship%20Project/tax_supervision_made_to_measure_tz0151z1fdeng.pdf (accessed 6 January 2017).

Commonwealth Association of Tax Administrators 2006. *Tax Evasion and Avoidance: Strategies and Initiatives for Tax Administrators*. London: Commonwealth Association of Tax Administrators.

Contini, B. 1981. "Labor market segmentation and the development of the parallel economy: the Italian experience". *Oxford Economic Papers* 33, 401–12.

Cook, D. 1997. *Poverty, Crime and Punishment*. London: Child Poverty Action Group.

Copisarow, R. 2004. *Street UK – A Micro-finance Organisation: Lessons Learned From its First Three Years' Operations*. Birmingham: Street UK.

Copisarow, R. & A. Barbour 2004. *Self-employed People in the Informal Economy: Cheats or Contributors?* London: Community Links.

Cornuel, D. & B. Duriez 1985. "Local exchange and state intervention". In N. Redclift & E. Mingione (eds), *Beyond Employment: Household, Gender and Subsistence*, 101–35. Oxford: Blackwell.

Crnkovic-Pozaic, S. 1999. "Measuring employment in the unofficial economy by using labor market data". In E. Feige & K. Ott (eds), *Underground Economies in Transition: Unrecorded Activity, Tax Evasion, Corruption and Organized Crime*, 120–32. Aldershot: Ashgate.

Cross, J. 2000. "Street vendors, modernity and postmodernity: conflict and compromise in the global economy". *International Journal of Sociology and Social Policy* 20(1), 29–51.

Cross, J. & A. Morales 2007. "Introduction: locating street markets in the modern/postmodern world". In J. Cross & A. Morales (eds), *Street Entrepreneurs*, 1–20. London: Routledge.

Cullis, J. & A. Lewis 1997. "Why do people pay taxes: from a conventional economic model to a model of social convention". *Journal of Economic Psychology* 18(2/3), 305–21.

Das, K. 2003. "Income and employment in informal manufacturing: a case study". In R. Jhabvala, R. Sudarshan & J. Unni (eds), *Informal Economy Centrestage: New Structures of Employment*, 42–69. London: Sage.

Davis, M. 2006. *Planet of Slums*. London: Verso.

De Beer, J., K. Fu & S. Wunsch-Vincent 2013. "The informal economy, innovation and intellectual property: concepts, metrics and policy considerations". Economic Research Working Paper no. 10. Geneva: World Intellectual Property Organization.

De Castro, J., S. Khavul & G. Bruton 2014. "Shades of grey: how do informal firms navigate between macro and meso institutional environments?". *Strategic Entrepreneurship Journal* 8, 75–94.

De Juan, A., M. Lasheras & R. Mayo 1994. "Voluntary tax compliant behavior of Spanish income taxpayers". *Public Finance* 49, 90–105.

De Mel, S., D. McKenzie & C. Woodruff 2012. "The demand for, and consequences of, formalization among informal firms in Sri Lanka". *American Economic Journal: Applied Economics* 5(2), 122–50.

De Soto, H. 1989. *The Other Path: The Invisible Revolution in the Third World*. New York: Harper & Row.

De Soto, H. 2001. *The Mystery of Capital: Why Capitalism Triumphs in the West and Fails Everywhere Else*. London: Black Swan.

Dekker, H. *et al.* 2010. *Joining Up the Fight Against Undeclared Work*. Brussels: DG Employment, Social Affairs and Equal Opportunities.

Del Boca, D. & F. Forte 1982. "Recent empirical surveys and theoretical interpretations of the parallel economy in Italy". In V. Tanzi (ed.), *The Underground Economy in the United States and Abroad*, 160–78. Lexington, MA: Lexington Books.

Dellot, B. 2012. *Untapped Enterprise: Learning to Live with the Informal Economy*. London: Royal Society of Arts.

Denzau, A. & D. North 1994. "Shared mental models: ideologies and institutions". *Kyklos* 47, 3–30.

Derrida, J. 1967. *Of Grammatology*. Baltimore, MD: Johns Hopkins University Press.

Devas, N. & R. Kelly 2001. "Regulation or revenue? An analysis of local business licenses, with a case study of the single business permit reform in Kenya". *Public Administration and Development* 21, 381–91.

Dibben, P. & C. Williams 2012. "Varieties of capitalism and employment relations: informally dominated market economies". *Industrial Relations: A Review of Economy & Society* 51(S1), 563–82.

Dibben, P., G. Wood & C. Williams 2015. "Towards and against formalization: regulation and change in informal work in Mozambique". *International Labour Review* 154(3), 373–92.

Dilnot, A. & C. Morris 1981. "What do we know about the black economy?". *Fiscal Studies* 2(1), 58–73.

Doane, D., D. Srikajon & R. Ofrenco 2003. "Social protection for informal workers in the garment industry". In F. Lund & J. Nicholson (eds), *Chains of Production, Ladders of Protection: Social Protection for Workers in the Informal Economy*, 101–42. Durban: School of Development Studies, University of Natal.

Dong, B., U. Dulleck & B. Torgler 2012. "Conditional corruption". *Journal of Economic Psychology* 33, 609–27.

Eurofound 2013. *Tackling Undeclared Work in 27 European Union Member States and Norway: Approaches and Measures Since 2008*. Dublin: Eurofound.

European Commission 1998. *Communication of the Commission on Undeclared Work*. Brussels: European Commission.

European Commission 2007. *Stepping up the Fight Against Undeclared Work*. Brussels: European Commission.

European Commission 2014a. *Employment and Social Developments in Europe 2013*. Brussels: European Commission.

European Commission 2014b. *Special Eurobarometer 402: Undeclared Work*. Brussels: European Commission.

European Commission 2016. Decision (EU) 2016/344 of the European Parliament and of the Council of 9 March 2016 on establishing a European Platform to enhance cooperation in tackling undeclared work. Brussels: European Commission.

Evans, M., S. Syrett & C. Williams 2006. *Informal Economic Activities and Deprived Neighbourhoods*. London: Department of Communities and Local Government.

Feige, E. 1979. "How big is the irregular economy?". *Challenge* 3(11/12), 5–13.

Feige, E. 2012. "The myth of the 'cashless society'? How much of America's currency is overseas". Available at: http://www.bundesbank.de/Redaktion/EN/Downloads/Core_business_areas/Cash_management/conferences/2012/2012_02_27_eltville_03_feige_paper.pdf?__blob=publicationFile (accessed 11 May 2017).

Feld, L. & B. Frey 2002. "Trust breeds trust: how taxpayers are treated". *Economics of Government* 3(2), 87–99.

Feld, L. & F. Schneider 2010. "Survey on the shadow economy and undeclared earnings in OECD countries". *German Economic Review* 11(2), 109–49.

Fernandez-Kelly, P. 2006. "Introduction". In P. Fernandez-Kelly & J. Shefner (eds), *Out of the Shadows: Political Action and the Informal Economy in Latin America*, 1–19. University Park, PA: Pennsylvania State University Press.

Ferreira, M. *et al.* 2012. "Unravelling the history of Brazilian Jeitinho: a cultural exploration of social norms". *Personality and Social Psychology Bulletin* 38(3), 331–44.

Fields, G. 1990. "Labour market modelling and the urban informal sector: theory and evidence". In D. Turnham, B. Salome & A. Schwarz (eds), *The Informal Sector Revisited*, 49–69. Paris: OECD.

Fields, G. 2005. "A guide to multisector labor market models". Social Protection discussion paper 0505. Washington, DC: World Bank.

Flaming, D., B. Haydamack & P. Joassart 2005. *Hopeful Workers, Marginal Jobs: LA's Off-the-Books Labor Force*. Los Angeles, CA: Economic Roundtable.

Fortin, B. *et al.* 1996. *L'economie souterraine au Quebec: mythes et realites*. Laval: Presses de l'Universite Laval.

Frey, B. 1997. *Not Just For Money: An Economic Theory of Personal Motivation*. Cheltenham: Elgar.

Frey, B. & H. Weck 1983. "Estimating the shadow economy: a 'naïve' approach". *Oxford Economic Papers* 35(1), 23–44.

Friedman, E. *et al.* 2000. "Dodging the grabbing hand: the determinants of unofficial activity in 69 countries". *Journal of Public Economics* 76(3), 459–93.

Fries, S., T. Lysenko & S. Polanec 2003. "The 2002 Business Environment and Enterprise Performance Survey: results from a survey of 6,100 firms". EBRD Working Paper no. 84. Available at: www.ebrd.com/pubs/find/index.html (accessed 6 June 2018).

Friman, H. 2004. "The great escape? Globalization, immigrant entrepreneurship and the criminal economy". *Review of International Political Economy* 11(1), 98–131.

Gallin, D. 2001. "Propositions on trade unions and informal employment in time of globalisation". *Antipode* 19(4), 531–49.

Gangl, K. *et al.* 2012. "The dynamics of power and trust in the 'slippery slope framework' and its impact on the tax climate". Available at http://papers/.ssrn.com/sol3/papers.cfm?abstract_id=2024946 (accessed 11 May 2017).

Garcia-Bolivar, O. 2006. *Informal Economy: Is it a Problem, a Solution or Both? The Perspective of the Informal Business*. Berkeley, CA: Bepress Legal Series.

Geertz, C. 1963. *Old Societies and New States: The Quest for Modernity in Asia and Africa*. Glencoe, IL: Free Press.

Gerxhani, K. 2004. "The informal sector in developed and less developed countries: a literature survey". *Public Choice* 120(3/4), 267–300.

GHK & Fondazione Brodolini 2009. *Study on Indirect Measurement Methods for Undeclared Work in the EU*. Brussels: European Commission.

Gilbert, A. 1998. *The Latin American City*. London: Latin American Bureau.

Giles, D. 1999a. "Measuring the hidden economy: implications for econometric modeling". *Economic Journal* 109(456), 370–80.

Giles, D. 1999b. "Modeling the hidden economy in the tax-gap in New Zealand". *Empirical Economics* 24(3), 621–40.

Giles, D. & L. Tedds 2002. *Taxes and the Canadian Underground Economy*. Toronto: Canadian Tax Foundation.

Godfrey, P. 2011. "Toward a theory of the informal economy". *Academy of Management Annals* 5(1), 231–77.

Godfrey, P. 2015. "Introduction: why the informal economy matters to management". In P. Godfrey (ed.), *Management, Society, and the Informal Economy*, 1–20. London: Routledge.

Grabiner, L. 2000. *The Informal Economy*. London: HM Treasury.

Gurtoo, A. & C. Williams 2009. "Entrepreneurship and the informal sector: some lessons from India". *International Journal of Entrepreneurship and Innovation* 10(1), 55–62.

Gutmann, P. 1977. "The subterranean economy". *Financial Analysts Journal* 34(1), 24–7.

Halla, M. 2010. "Tax morale and compliance behaviour: first evidence on a causal link". IZA discussion paper 4918. Bonn: IZA.

Harriss-White, B. 2014. "Labour and petty production". *Development and Change* 45(5), 981–1000.

Harriss-White, B. 2017. "Formality and informality in an Indian urban waste economy". *International Journal of Sociology and Social Policy* 37(7/8), 121–42.

Hart, K. 1973. "Informal income opportunities and urban employment in Ghana". *Journal of Modern African Studies* 11(1), 61–89.

Hartner, M. *et al.* 2008. "Procedural justice and tax compliance". *Economic Analysis and Policy* 38(1), 137–52.

Hasseldine, J. & Z. Li 1999. "More tax evasion research required in new millennium". *Crime, Law and Social Change* 31(1), 91–104.

Hellberger, C. & J. Schwarze 1986. *Umfang und struktur der nebenerwerbstatigkeit in der Bundesrepublik Deutschland*. Berlin: Mitteilungen aus der Arbeits-market- und Berufsforschung.

Helmke, G. & S. Levitsky 2004. "Informal institutions and comparative politics: a research agenda". *Perspectives on Politics* 2(6), 725–40.

Henry, J. 1976. "Calling in the big bills". *Washington Monthly* 5, 6.

Hill, R. & M. Kabir 1996. "Tax rates, the tax mix, and the growth of the underground economy in Canada: what can we infer?". *Canadian Tax Journal/Revue Fiscale Canadienne* 64(6), 1552–83.

Hodosi, A. 2015. "Perceptions of irregular immigrants' participation in undeclared work in the United Kingdom from a social trust perspective". *International Journal of Sociology and Social Policy* 35(5/6), 375–89.

Horodnic, I. 2016. *Cash Wage Payments in Transition Economies: Consequences of Envelope Wages*. Bonn: IZA.

Hudson, R. 2005. *Economic Geographies: Circuits, Flows and Spaces*. London: Sage.

Hussmanns, R. 2005. "Measuring the informal economy: from employment in the informal sector to informal employment". ILO Policy Integration Department/Bureau of Statistics, working paper 53. Geneva: ILO.

International Labour Organization (ILO) 2002a. *Decent Work and the Informal Economy*. Geneva: ILO.

International Labour Organization (ILO) 2002b. *Women and Men in the Informal Economy: A Statistical Picture*. Geneva: ILO.

International Labour Organization (ILO) 2011. *Statistical Update on Employment in the Informal Economy*. Geneva: ILO.

International Labour Organization (ILO) 2012. *Statistical Update on Employment in the Informal Economy*. Geneva: ILO.

International Labour Organization (ILO) 2013. *Women and Men in the Informal Economy: Statistical Picture*. Geneva: ILO.

International Labour Organization (ILO) 2014. *Transitioning from the Informal to the Formal Economy*. Geneva: ILO.

International Labour Organization (ILO) 2015. *Recommendation 204 Concerning the Transition from the Informal to the Formal Economy*. Geneva: ILO.

International Labour Organization (ILO) 2017. *ILO Approach to Strategic Compliance for Labour Inspectorates*. Geneva: ILO.

Isachsen, A., J. Klovland & S. Strom 1982. "The hidden economy in Norway". In V. Tanzi (ed.), *The Underground Economy in the United States and Abroad*, 209–31. Lexington, MA: D. C. Heath.

Itzigsohn, J. 2000. *Developing Poverty: The State, Labor Market Deregulation and the Informal Economy in Costa Rica and the Dominican Republic*. University Park, PA: Pennsylvania State University Press.

Jaramillo, M. 2009. "Is there demand for formality among informal firms? Evidence from microfirms in downtown Lima". German Development Institute discussion paper 12/2009. Bonn: German Development Institute.

Jensen, L., G. Cornwell & J. Findeis 1995. "Informal work in nonmetropolitan Pennsylvania". *Rural Sociology* 60(1), 91–107.

Job, J., A. Stout & R. Smith 2007. "Culture change in three taxation administrations: from command and control to responsive regulation". *Law and Policy* 29(1), 84–101.

Johnson, S., D. Kaufmann & A. Shleifer 1997. "The unofficial economy in transition". *Brookings Papers on Economic Activity* 2, 159–239.

Johnson, S., D. Kaufmann & P. Zoido-Lobatón 1998. "Regulatory discretion and the unofficial economy". *American Economic Review* 88(2), 387–92.

Jones, T., M. Ram & P. Edwards 2004. "Illegal immigrants and the informal economy: worker and employer experiences in the Asian underground economy". *International Journal of Economic Development* 6(1), 92–106.

Karjanen, D. 2011. "Tracing informal and illicit flows after socialism: a micro-commodity supply chain analysis in the Slovak Republic". *International Journal of Sociology and Social Policy* 31(11/12), 648–63.

Karki, S. & M. Xheneti 2018. "Formalizing women entrepreneurs in Kathmandu, Nepal: pathway towards empowerment?". *International Journal of Sociology and Social Policy* 38(7/8), 526–40.

Karlinger, L. 2013. "The 'dark side' of deregulation: how competition affects the size of the shadow economy". *Journal of Public Economic Theory* 16(2), 283–321.

Karpuskiene, V. 2007. "Undeclared work, tax evasion and avoidance in Lithuania". Paper presented at colloquium of the Belgian Federal Service for Social Security on Undeclared Work, Tax Evasion and Avoidance, Brussels.

Katungi, D., E. Neale & A. Barbour 2006. *People in Low-Paid Informal Work*. York: Rowntree Foundation.

Kempson, E. 1996. *Life on a Low Income*. York: York Publishing Services.

Kesteloot, C. & H. Meert 1999. "Informal spaces: the geography of informal economic activities in Brussels". *International Journal of Urban and Regional Research* 23(2), 232–51.

Ketchen, D., R. Ireland & J. Webb 2014. "Towards a research agenda for the informal economy: a survey of the *Strategic Entrepreneurship Journal*'s Editorial Board". *Strategic Entrepreneurship Journal* 8, 95–100.

Khan, E. 2017. "An investigation of marketing capabilities of informal microenterprises: a study of street food vending in Thailand". *International Journal of Sociology and Social Policy* 37(3/4), 186–202.

Khan, E. & M. Quaddus 2015. "Examining the influence of business environment on socio-economic performance of informal microenterprises: content analysis and partial least square approach". *International Journal of Sociology and Social Policy* 35(3/4), 273–88.

Kinsey, K. & H. Gramsick 1993. "Did the tax reform act of 1986 improve compliance? Three studies of pre- and post-TRA compliance attitudes". *Law and Policy* 15, 239–325.

Kirchler, E. 1997. "The burden of new taxes: acceptance of taxes as a function of affectedness and egoistic versus altruistic orientation". *Journal of Socio-Economics* 26, 421–36.

Kirchler, E. 1998. "Differential representations of taxes: analysis of free associations and judgments of five employment groups". *Journal of Socio-Economics* 27, 117–31.

Kirchler, E. 1999. "Reactance to taxation: employers' attitudes towards taxes". *Journal of Socio-Economics* 28, 131–8.

Kirchler, E. 2007. *The Economic Psychology of Tax Behaviour*. Cambridge: Cambridge University Press.

Kirchler, E., E. Hoelzl & I. Wahl 2008. "Enforced versus voluntary tax compliance: the 'slippery slope' framework". *Journal of Economic Psychology* 29, 210–25.

Kistruck, G. *et al.* 2015. "The double-edged sword of legitimacy in base-of-the-pyramid markets". *Journal of Business Venturing* 30(3), 436–51.

Kogler, C., S. Muelbacher & E. Kirchler 2015. "Testing the 'slippery slope framework' among self-employed taxpayers". *Economics of Governance* 16, 125–41.

Kogler, C. *et al.* 2013. "Trust and power as determinants of tax compliance: testing the assumptions of the slippery slope framework in Austria, Hungary, Romania and Russia". *Journal of Economic Psychology* 34, 169–80.

Komter, A. 1996. "Reciprocity as a principle of exclusion: gift giving in the Netherlands". *Sociology* 30(2), 299–316.

Kovács, B. 2014. "Nannies and informality in Romanian local childcare markets". In J. Morris & A. Polese (eds), *The Informal Post-Socialist Economy: Embedded Practices and Livelihoods*, 67–84. Abingdon: Routledge.

Kukk, M. & K. Staehr 2014. "Income underreporting by households with business income: evidence from Estonia". *Post-Communist Economies* 26, 226–57.

La Porta, R. & A. Shleifer 2008. "The unofficial economy and economic development". *Brookings Papers on Economic Activity* 47(1), 123–35.

La Porta, R. & A. Shleifer 2014. "Informality and development". *Journal of Economic Perspectives* 28(3), 109–26.

Lackó, M. 1999. "Electricity intensity and the unrecorded economy in post-socialist countries". In E. Feige & K. Ott (eds), *Underground Economies in Transition*, 102–42. Aldershot: Ashgate.

Lagos, R. 1995. "Formalising the informal sector: barriers and costs". *Development and Change* 26(1), 110–31.

Langfeldt, E. 1984. "The unobserved economy in the Federal Republic of Germany". In E. Feige (ed.), *The Unobserved Economy*, 236–60. Cambridge: Cambridge University Press.

Larsen, L. 2013a. "The making of a good deal". *Journal of Cultural Economy* 6(4), 419–33.

Larsen, L. 2013b. "Buy or barter? Illegal yet licit purchases of work in contemporary Sweden". *Focaal: Journal of Global and Historical Anthropology* 66, 75–87.

Leal Ordóñez, J. 2014. "Tax collection, the informal sector and productivity". *Review of Economic Dynamics* 17, 262–86.

Ledeneva, A. 2013. *Can Russia Modernise? Sistema, Power Networks and Informal Governance*. Cambridge: Cambridge University Press.

Lemieux, T., B. Fortin & P. Frechette 1994. "The effect of taxes on labour supply in the underground economy". *American Economic Review* 84(1), 231–54.

Leonard, M. 1994. *Informal Economic Activity in Belfast*. Aldershot: Avebury.

Leonard, M. 1998. *Invisible Work, Invisible Workers: The Informal Economy in Europe and the US*. London: Macmillan Press.

Levitsky, S. & M. Murillo 2009. "Variation in institutional strength". *Annual Review of Political Science* 12(1), 115–33.

Levy, S. 2008. *Good Intentions, Bad Outcomes: Social Policy, Informality and Economic Growth in Mexico*. Washington, DC: Brookings Institution.

Lewis, A. 1954. "Economic development with unlimited supplies of labor". *Manchester School of Economics and Social Studies* 22(1), 139–91.

Lewis, A. 1959. *The Theory of Economic Growth*. London: Allen & Unwin.

Lewis, A. 1982. *The Psychology of Taxation*. Oxford: Martin Robertson.

Lewis, W. 2004. *The Power of Productivity: Wealth, Poverty, and the Threat to Global Stability*. Chicago, IL: University of Chicago Press.

Lin, S. 2018. "'We work like ants … we avoid being troublemaker': an exploratory inquiry on resilience of Chinese street vendors in the urban village". *International Journal of Sociology and Social Policy* 38(11/12), 1024–40.

Linares, L. 2018. "The paradoxes of informalizing street trade in the Latin American city". *International Journal of Sociology and Social Policy*, 38(7/8), 651–72.

Little, P. 2003. *Somalia: Economy Without State*. Bloomington, IN: Indiana University Press.

Llanes, M. & A. Barbour 2007. *Self-Employed and Micro-Entrepreneurs: Informal Trading and the Journey towards Formalization*. London: Community Links.

Loayza, N. 2007. "The causes and consequences of informality in Peru". Working Paper 18. Lima: Banco Central de Reserva del Perú.

Lobo, F. 1990. "Irregular work in Spain". In *Underground Economy and Irregular Forms of Employment, Final Synthesis Report*. Brussels: Office for Official Publications of the European Communities.

London, T. & S. Hart 2004. "Reinventing strategies for emerging markets: beyond the transnational model". *Journal of International Business Studies* 35(5), 350–70.

London, T. *et al.* 2014. "Connecting poverty to purchase in informal markets". *Strategic Entrepreneurship Journal* 8, 37–55.

MacAfee, K. 1980. "A glimpse of the hidden economy in the national accounts". *Economic Trends* 136, 81–7.

MacDonald, R. 1994. "Fiddly jobs, undeclared working and the something for nothing society". *Work, Employment and Society* 8(4), 507–30.

Mair, J., I. Marti & M. Ventresca 2012. "Building inclusive markets in rural Bangladesh: how intermediaries work institutional voids". *Academy of Management Journal* 55, 819–50.

Maldonado, C. 1995. "The informal sector: legalization or laissez-faire?" *International Labour Review* 134(6), 705–28.

Maloney, W. 2004. "Informality revisited". *World Development* 32(7), 1159–78.

Mateman, S. & P. Renooy 2001. *Undeclared Labour in Europe: Towards an Integrated Approach of Combating Undeclared Labour*. Amsterdam: Regioplan.

Mathias, B. *et al*. 2014. "Competing against the unknown: the impact of enabling and constraining institutions on the informal economy". *Journal of Business Ethics* 127(2), 251–64.

Mattera, P. 1985. *Off the Books: The Rise of the Underground Economy*. New York: St Martin's Press.

Matthews, K. 1982. "The demand for currency and the black economy in the UK". *Journal of Economic Studies* 9(2), 3–22.

Matthews, K. 1983. "National income and the black economy". *Journal of Economic Affairs* 3(4), 261–67.

Matthews, K. & A. Rastogi 1985. "Little mo and the moonlighters: another look at the black economy". *Quarterly Economic Bulletin* 6, 21–4.

McGee, R., J. Alver & L. Alver 2008. "The ethics of tax evasion: a survey of Estonian opinion". In R.W. McGee (ed.), *Taxation and Public Finance in Transition and Developing Countries*, 119–36. Berlin: Springer.

McInnis-Dittrich, K. 1995. "Women of the shadows: Appalachian women's participation in the informal economy". *Affilia: Journal of Women and Social Work* 10(4), 398–412.

Meagher, K. 2010. *Identity Economics: Social Networks and the Informal Economy in Nigeria*. London: James Currey.

Meriküll, J. & K. Staehr 2010. "Unreported employment and envelope wages in mid-transition: comparing developments and causes in the Baltic countries". *Comparative Economic Studies* 52(3), 637–70.

Mešić, N. 2016. "Paradoxes of European free movement in times of austerity: the role of social movement actors in framing the plight of Roma berry pickers in Sweden". *International Journal of Sociology and Social Policy* 36(5/6), 289–303.

Molero, J. & F. Pujol 2012. "Walking inside the potential tax evader's mind: tax morale does matter". *Journal of Business Ethics* 105, 151–62.

Morissette, C. 2014. *The Underground Economy in Canada, 1992 to 2011*. Vancouver: Statistics Canada.

Morris, L. 1994. "Informal aspects of social divisions". *International Journal of Urban and Regional Research* 18(1), 112–26.

Morris, J. & A. Polese 2014. "Introduction: informality – enduring practices, entwined livelihoods". In J. Morris & A. Polese (eds), *The Informal Post-Socialist Economy: Embedded Practices and Livelihoods*, 1–18. Abingdon: Routledge.

Moser, C. 1977. "The dual economy and marginality debate and the contribution of micro analysis: market sellers in Bogotá". *Development and Change* 8(4), 465–89.

Müller, E. 2012. "Fair play: fairness *zahlt sich aus* [fairness pays]". Lecture presented at the meeting of the Austrian Science Fund, Vienna, 6 July.

Müller, K. & J. Miggelbrink 2014. "The glove compartment half full of letters: informality and cross-border trade at the edge of the Schengen area". In J. Morris & A. Polese (eds), *The Informal Post-Socialist Economy*, 151–64. London: Routledge.

Murphy, K. 2003. "Procedural fairness and tax compliance". *Australian Journal of Social Issues* 38(3), 379–408.

Murphy, K. 2005. "Regulating more effectively: the relationship between procedural justice, legitimacy and tax non-compliance". *Journal of Law and Society* 32(4), 562–89.

Murphy, K. 2008. "Enforcing tax compliance: to punish or persuade?". *Economic Analysis and Policy* 38(1), 113–35.

Murphy, K. & N. Harris 2007. "Shaming, shame and recidivism: a test of re-integrative shaming theory in the white-collar crime context". *British Journal of Criminology* 47, 900–17.

Murphy, K., T. Tyler & A. Curtis 2009. "Nurturing regulatory compliance: is procedural fairness effective when people question the legitimacy of the law?". *Regulation and Governance* 3, 1–26.

Neef, R. 2002. "Aspects of the informal economy in a transforming country: the case of Romania". *International Journal of Urban and Regional Research* 26(2), 299–322.

Nelson, E. & E. Bruijn 2005. "The voluntary formation of enterprises in a developing economy: the case of Tanzania". *Journal of International Development* 17, 575–93.

Nelson, M. & J. Smith 1999. *Working Hard and Making Do: Surviving in Small Town America*. Los Angeles, CA: University of California Press.

North, D. 1990. *Institution, Institutional Change and Economic Performance*. Cambridge: Cambridge University Press.

Nwabuzor, A. 2005. "Corruption and development: new initiatives in economic openness and strengthened rule of law". *Journal of Business Ethics* 59(1/2), 121–38.

O'Higgins, M. 1989. "Assessing the underground economy in the United Kingdom". In E. Feige (ed.), *The Underground Economies*, 175–95. Cambridge: Cambridge University Press.

OECD 2002. *Measuring the Non-Observed Economy*. Paris: OECD.

OECD 2008. *OECD Employment Outlook*. Paris: OECD.

OECD 2012. *Reducing Opportunities for Tax Non-Compliance in the Underground Economy*. Paris: OECD.

OECD 2013. *Co-operative Compliance: A Framework from Enhanced Relationship to Co-operative Compliance*. Available at: http://www.oecd.org/ctp/administration/co-operativecompliance.htm. (accessed 6 July 2016)

OECD 2016. *Informal Sector Entrepreneurship: A Policy Briefing*. Paris: OECD.

Ojo, S., S. Nwankwo & A. Gbadamosi 2013. "Ethnic entrepreneurship: the myths of informal and illegal enterprise in the UK". *Entrepreneurship and Regional Development* 25(7/8), 587–611.

Ostapenko, N. & C. Williams 2016. "Determinants of entrepreneurs' views on the acceptability of tax evasion and the informal economy in Slovakia and Ukraine: an institutional asymmetry approach". *International Journal of Entrepreneurship and Small Business* 28(2/3), 120–42.

Otero, M. 1994. "The role of governments and private institutions in addressing the informal sector in Latin America". In C. Rakowski (ed.), *Contrapunto: The Informal Sector Debate in Latin America*, 129–42. New York: SUNY Press.

Packard, T. 2007. *Do Workers in Chile Choose Informal Employment? A Dynamic Analysis of Sector Choice*. Washington, DC: World Bank Latin American and the Caribbean Region Social Projection Unit.

Paglin, M. 1994. "The underground economy: new estimates from household income and expenditure surveys". *Yale Law Journal* 103(8), 2239–57.

Pahl, R. 1984. *Divisions of Labour*. Oxford: Blackwell.

Perry, G. & W Maloney 2007. "Overview: informality – exit and exclusion". In G. Perry *et al.* (eds), *Informality: Exit and Exclusion*, 1–20. Washington, DC: World Bank.

Petersen, L. & A. Charman 2018. "The role of family in the township informal economy of food and drink in KwaMashu, South Africa". *International Journal of Sociology and Social Policy* 38(7/8), 564–77.

Piore, M. & C. Sabel 1984. *The Second Industrial Divide*. New York: Basic Books.

Pommerehne, W. & H. Weck-Hannemann 1996. "Tax rates, tax administration, and income tax evasion in Switzerland". *Public Choice* 88, 161–70.

Pope, J. 2000. *Confronting Corruption: The Elements of a National Integrity System*. Berlin: Transparency International.

Portes, A. 1994. "The informal economy and its paradoxes". In N. Smelser & R. Swedberg (eds), *The Handbook of Economic Sociology*, 142–65. Princeton, NJ: Princeton University Press.

Portes, A. & S. Sassen-Koob 1987. "Making it underground: comparative material on the informal sector in Western market economies". *American Journal of Sociology* 93(1), 30–61.

Potts, D. 2008. "The urban *informal* sector in sub-Saharan Africa: from bad to good (and back again?)". *Development Southern Africa* 25(2), 151–67.

Purdam, K. & M. Tranmer 2014. "Expectations of being helped in return for helping: citizens, the state and the local area". *Population, Space and Place* 20, 66–82.

Putniņš, T. & A. Sauka 2015. "Measuring the shadow economy using company managers". *Journal of Comparative Economics* 43, 471–90.

Rakowski, C. 1994a. "Convergence and divergence in the informal sector debate: a focus on Latin America, 1984–92". *World Development* 22(4), 501–16.

Rakowski, C. 1994b. "The informal sector debate, part II: 1984–1993". In C. Rakowski (ed.), *Contrapunto*, 121–52. New York: SUNY Press.

Ram, M., P. Edwards & T. Jones 2002. *Employers and Illegal Migrant Workers in the Clothing and Restaurant Sectors*. London: DTI Central Unit Research.

Ram, M., P. Edwards & T. Jones 2007. "Staying underground: informal work, small firms and employment regulation in the United Kingdom". *Work and Occupations* 34(3), 318–44.

Ram, M. *et al.* 2001. "The dynamics of informality: employment relations in small firms and the effects of regulatory change". *Work, Employment and Society* 15(4), 845–61.

Ram, M. *et al.* 2002. "Ethnic minority enterprise in its urban context: South Asian restaurants in Birmingham". *International Journal of Urban and Regional Research* 26(1), 24–40.

Ram, M. *et al.* 2003. "Once more into the sunset? Asian clothing firms after the national minimum wage". *Environment and Planning C: Government and Policy* 71(3), 238–61.

Ramas, R. 2016. "Parental informal payments in Kyrgyzstani schools: analyzing the strongest and the weakest link". *Journal of Eurasian Studies* 7, 205–19.

Renooy, P. 1990. *The Informal Economy: Meaning, Measurement and Social Significance*. Netherlands Geographical Studies no. 115. Utrecht: Royal Dutch Geographical Society.

Renooy, P. *et al.* 2004. *Undeclared Work in an Enlarged Union: An Analysis of Shadow Work: An In-depth Study of Specific Items*. Brussels: European Commission.

Riahi-Belkaoui, A. 2004. "Relationship between tax compliance internationally and selected determinants of tax morale". *Journal of International Accounting, Auditing and Taxation* 13(2), 135–43.

Richardson, G. 2006. "Determinants of tax evasion: a cross-country investigation". *Journal of International Accounting, Auditing and Taxation* 15(2), 150–69.

Richardson, M. & A. Sawyer 2001. "A taxonomy of the tax compliance literature: further findings, problems and prospects". *Australian Tax Forum* 16(2), 137–320.

Round, J. & C. Williams 2008. "Everyday tactics and spaces of power: the role of informal economies in post-Soviet Ukraine". *Social and Cultural Geography* 9(2), 171–85.

Round, J., C. Williams & P. Rodgers 2008. "Corruption in the post-Soviet workplace: the experiences of recent graduates in contemporary Ukraine". *Work, Employment and Society* 22(1), 149–66.

Sasaki, S., K. Kyoko Kusakabe & P. Doneys 2016. "Exploring human (in-)security from a gender perspective: a case study of subcontracted workers in Thailand". *International Journal of Sociology and Social Policy* 36(5/6), 304–18.

Sassen, S. 1996. "Service employment regimes and the new inequality". In E. Mingione (ed.), *Urban Poverty and the Underclass*, 142–59. Oxford: Blackwell.

Sassen, S. 1997. "Informalisation in advanced market economies". Issues in Development discussion paper 20. Geneva: International Labour Organisation.

Sasunkevich, O. 2014. "Business as casual: shuttle trade on the Belarus–Lithuania border". In J. Morris & A. Polese (eds), *The Informal Post-Socialist Economy*. 135–51. Abingdon: Routledge.

Sauka, A., F. Schneider & C. Williams (eds) 2016. *Entrepreneurship and the Shadow Economy: A European Perspective*. Cheltenham: Elgar.

Sauvy, A. 1984. *Le travail noir et l'économie de demain*. Paris: Calmann-Levy.

Schanz, G. von 1890. *Die steuern der schweiz in ihrer entwicklung seit beginn des 19 jahrhunderts, Vols I–V*. Stuttgart: Rowolt.

Schmölders, G. 1952. "Finanzpsychologie". *Finanzarchiv* 13, 1–36.

Schmölders, G. 1960. *Das irrationale in der öffentlichen finanzwissenschaft*. Hamburg: Rowolt.

Schmölders, G. 1962. *Volkswirtschaftslehre und psychologie*. Berlin: Reinbek.

Schneider F. 2001. "What do we know about the shadow economy? Evidence from 21 OECD countries". *World Economics* 2(4), 19–32.

Schneider, F. 2002. "Size and measurement of the informal economy in 110 countries around the world". Paper presented at a workshop of Australian National Tax Centre, ANU, Canberra, July.

Schneider, F. 2005. "Shadow economies around the world: what do we really know". *European Journal of Political Economy* 21(3), 598–642.

Schneider, F. 2013. "Size and development of the shadow economy of 31 European and 5 other OECD countries from 2003 to 2013: a further decline". Available at: http://www.econ.jku.at/members/Schneider/files/publications/2013/ShadEcEurope31_Jan2013.pdf (accessed 6 August 2017).

Schneider, F., A. Buehn & C. Montenegro 2010. "New estimates for the shadow economies all over the world". *International Economic Journal* 24(4), 443–61.

Schneider, F. & D. Enste 2000. "Shadow economies: size, causes, and consequences". *Journal of Economic Literature* 38(1), 77–114.

Schneider, F. & D. Enste 2002. *The Shadow Economy: Theoretical Approaches, Empirical Studies, and Political Implications*. Cambridge: Cambridge University Press.

Schneider, F. & R. Klinglmair 2004. "Shadow economies around the world: what do we know?". IZA discussion paper 1043. Bonn: IZA.

Schneider, F. & C. Williams 2013. *The Shadow Economy*. London: Institute of Economic Affairs.

Scott, W. 2008. *Institutions and Organizations: Ideas and Interests*. London: Sage.

Sedlenieks, K. 2003. "Cash in an envelope: corruption and tax avoidance as an economic strategy in Contemporary Riga". In K.-O. Arnstberg & T. Boren (eds), *Everyday Economy in Russia, Poland and Latvia*, 42–62. Stockholm: Almqvist & Wiksell.

Sepulveda, L. & S. Syrett 2007. "Out of the shadows? Formalisation approaches to informal economic activity". *Policy and Politics* 35(1), 87–104.

Shaw, J., J. Slemrod & J. Whiting 2008. *Administration and Compliance*. London: Institute for Fiscal Studies.

Shleifer, A. & R. Vishny 1993. "Corruption". *Quarterly Journal of Economics* 108, 599–617.

Siqueira, A., J. Webb & G. Bruton 2016. "Informal entrepreneurship and industry conditions". *Entrepreneurship Theory and Practice* 40(1), 177–200.

Slack, T. *et al.* 2017. "Social embeddedness, formal labor supply, and participation in informal work". *International Journal of Sociology and Social Policy* 37(3/4), 248–64.

Slavnic, Z. 2010. "Political economy of informalisation". *European Societies* 12(1), 3–23.

Slemrod, J., M. Blumenthal & C. Christian 2001. "Taxpayer response to an increased probability of audit: evidence from a controlled experiment in Minnesota". *Journal of Public Economics* 79, 455–83.

Small Business Council 2004. *Small Business in the Informal Economy: Making the Transition to the Formal Economy*. London: Small Business Council.

Smith, J. 1985. "Market motives in the informal economy". In W. Gaertner & A. Wenig (eds), *The Economics of the Shadow Economy*, 161–77. Heidelberg: Springer.

Smith, P. *et al.* 2011. "Are indigenous approaches to achieving influence in business organizations distinctive? A comparative study of guanxi, wasta, jeitinho, svyazi and pulling strings". *International Journal of Human Resource Management* 23(2), 333–48.

Smith, P. *et al.* 2012. "How distinctive are indigenous ways of achieving influence? A comparative study of guanxi, wasta, jeitinho, svyazi and pulling strings". *Journal of Cross-Cultural Psychology*, 43(1), 135–50.

Snijders, T. & R. Bosker 2012. *Multilevel Analysis: An Introduction to Basic and Advanced Multilevel Modelling*. London: Sage.

Snyder, K. 2004. "Routes to the informal economy in New York's East Village: crisis, economics and identity". *Sociological Perspectives* 47(2), 215–40.

Social Progress Imperative 2014. *Social Progress Index*. Available at: http://www.social progressimperative.org/ (accessed 19 December 2017).

Spandler, H. *et al.* 2014. *Informal Support in a Yorkshire Town: Interim Findings*. York: Rowntree Foundation.

Stănculescu, M. 2005. "Working conditions in the informal sector". *South East Europe Review for Labour and Social Affairs* 10(3), 79–93.

Staudt, K. 1998. *Free Trade? Informal Economies at the US–Mexico Border*. Philadelphia, PA: Temple University Press.

Strümpel, B. 1969. "The contribution of survey research to public finance". In A. Peacock (ed.), *Quantitative Analysis in Public Finance*, 12–32. New York: Praeger.

Svensson, J. 2005. "Eight questions about corruption". *Journal of Economic Perspectives* 19, 19–42.

Taiwo, O. 2013. "Employment choice and mobility in multi-sector labour markets: theoretical model and evidence from Ghana". *International Labour Review* 152(3/4), 469–92.

Tanzi, V. 1980. "The underground economy in the United States: estimates and implications". *Banca Nazionale del Lavoro* 135, 427–53.

Tanzi, V. 1999. "Uses and abuses of estimates of the underground economy". *Economic Journal* 109(456), 338–47.

Thai, M. & E. Turkina 2014. "Macro-level determinants of formal entrepreneurship versus informal entrepreneurship". *Journal of Business Venturing* 29(4), 490–510.

Thomas, J. 1986. "The underground economy in the United States: comment on Tanzi". *IMF Staff Papers* 33, 782–9.

Thomas, J. 1992. *Informal Economic Activity*. Hemel Hempstead: Harvester Wheatsheaf.

Thurman, Q., C. St. John & L. Riggs 1984. "Neutralisation and tax evasion: how effective would a moral appeal be in improving compliance to tax laws?". *Law and Policy* 6(3), 309–27.

Tokman, V. 2001. "Integrating the informal sector in the modernization process". *SAIS Review* 21(1), 45–60.

Tonoyan, V. *et al.* 2010. "Corruption and entrepreneurship: how formal and informal institutions shape small firm behaviour in transition and mature market economies". *Entrepreneurship Theory and Practice* 34(5), 803–31.

Torgler, B. 2003. "To evade taxes or not: that is the question". *Journal of Socio-Economics* 32, 283–302.

Torgler, B. 2005a. "Tax morale in Latin America". *Public Choice* 122, 133–57.

Torgler, B. 2005b. "Tax morale and direct democracy". *European Journal of Political Economy* 21, 525–31.

Torgler, B. 2006a. *Tax Compliance and Tax Morale: A Theoretical and Empirical Analysis*. Cheltenham: Elgar.

Torgler, B. 2006b. "The importance of faith: tax morale and religiosity". *Journal of Economic Behavior and Organization* 61(1), 81–109.

Torgler, B. 2007. "Tax morale in Central and Eastern European countries". In N. Hayoz & S. Hug (eds), *Tax Evasion, Trust and State Capacities: How Good is Tax Morale in Central and Eastern Europe?*, 155–86. Bern: Peter Lang.

Torgler, B. 2011. "Tax morale and compliance: review of evidence and case studies for Europe". World Bank policy research working paper 5922. Washington, DC: World Bank.

Torgler, B. & F. Schneider 2009. "The impact of tax morale and institutional quality on the shadow economy". *Journal of Economic Psychology* 30, 228–45.

Transparency International 2013. Corruption Perceptions Index (CPI). Available at: http://www.transparency.org/research/cpi (accessed 10 January 2018).

Travers, A. 2002. *Prospects for Enterprise: An Investigation into the Motivations of Workers in the Informal Economy*. London: Community Links.

Trundle, J. 1982. "Recent changes in the use of cash". *Bank of England Quarterly Bulletin* 22, 519–29.

Trades Union Congress (TUC) 2008. *Hard Work, Hidden Lives: The Short Report of the Commission on Vulnerable Employment*. London: TUC.

Tyler, T. *et al.* 2007. "Reintegrative shaming, procedural justice and recidivism: the engagement of offenders' psychological mechanisms in the Canberra RISE drinking and driving experiment". *Law and Society Review* 41, 533–86.

Unai, J. & U. Rani 2003. "Employment and income in the informal economy: a micro-perspective". In R. Jhabvala, R. Sudarshan & J. Unni (eds), *Informal Economy Centrestage: New Structures of Employment*, 142–69. London: Sage.

United Nations Development Programme 2014. *Human Development Index and its Components*. Available at: http://hdr.undp.org/en/data (accessed 14 May 2018).

US Congress Joint Economic Committee 1983. *Growth of the Underground Economy 1950–81*. Washington, DC: Government Printing Office.

US General Accounting Office 1989. *Sweatshops in New York City: A Local Example of a Nationwide Problem*. Washington, DC: US General Accounting Office.

Vainio, A. 2012. *Market-Based and Rights-Based Approaches to the Informal Economy: A Comparative Analysis of the Policy Implications*. Oslo: Nordiska Afrijainstitutet.

Van Geuns, R., J. Mevissen & P. Renooy 1987. "The spatial and sectoral diversity of the informal economy". *Tijdschrift voor Economische en Sociale Geografie* 78(5), 389–98.

Vanderseypen, G. *et al.* 2013. "Undeclared work: recent developments". In European Commission (ed.), *Employment and Social Developments in Europe 2013*, 231–74. Brussels: European Commission.

Villaries-Varela, M. *et al.* 2017. "From the informal economy to the meaning of informality: developing theory on firms and their workers". *International Journal of Sociology and Social Policy* 37(7/8), 42–65.

Wallace, C. & R. Latcheva 2006. "Economic transformation outside the law: corruption, trust in public institutions and the informal economy in transition countries of Central and Eastern Europe". *Europe–Asia Studies* 58, 81–102.

Webb, J. & R. Ireland 2015. "Laying the foundation for a theory of informal adjustments". In P. Godfrey (ed.), *Management, Society, and the Informal Economy*, 21–41. Abingdon: Routledge.

Webb, J., R. Ireland & D. Ketchen 2014. "Toward a greater understanding of entrepreneurship and strategy in the informal economy". *Strategic Entrepreneurship Journal* 8, 1–15.

Webb, J. *et al.* 2009. "You say illegal, I say legitimate: entrepreneurship in the informal economy". *Academy of Management Review* 34(3), 492–510.

Webb, J. *et al.* 2013. "Research on entrepreneurship in the informal economy: framing a research agenda". *Journal of Business Venturing* 28(5), 598–614.

Weck-Hanneman, H. & B. Frey 1985. "Measuring the shadow economy: the case of Switzerland". In W. Gaertner & A. Wenig (eds), *The Economics of the Shadow Economy*, 142–65. Berlin: Springer.

Weigel, R., D. Hessin & H. Elffers 1987. "Tax evasion research: a critical appraisal and theoretical model". *Journal of Economic Psychology* 8(2), 215–35.

Welter, F., D. Smallbone & A. Pobol 2015. "Entrepreneurial activity in the informal economy: a missing piece of the jigsaw puzzle". *Entrepreneurship and Regional Development* 27(5/6), 292–306.

Wenzel, M. 2002. "The impact of outcome orientation and justice concerns on tax compliance: the role of taxpayers' identity". *Journal of Applied Psychology* 87, 639–45.

Wenzel, M. 2004. "An analysis of norm processes in tax compliance". *Journal of Economic Psychology* 25(2), 213–28.

White, R. & C. Williams 2010. "Re-thinking monetary exchange: some lessons from England". *Review of Social Economy* 68, 317–38.

Williams, C. 2001. "Tackling the participation of the unemployed in paid informal work: a critical evaluation of the deterrence approach". *Environment and Planning C* 19(5), 729–49.

Williams, C. 2003. "Developing voluntary activity: some policy lessons from the 2001 Home Office Citizenship Survey". *Social Policy and Society* 2(4), 285–94.

Williams, C. 2004a. "Harnessing enterprise and entrepreneurship in the underground economy". *International Journal of Economic Development* 6(2), 23–54.

Williams, C. 2004b. "Beyond deterrence: rethinking the UK public policy approach towards undeclared work". *Public Policy and Administration* 19(1), 15–30.

Williams, C. 2004c. *Cash-in-hand Work: The Underground Sector and the Hidden Economy of Favours*. Basingstoke: Palgrave Macmillan.

Williams, C. 2006a. *The Hidden Enterprise Culture: Entrepreneurship in the Underground Economy*. Cheltenham: Elgar.

Williams, C. 2006b. "What is to be done about undeclared work? An evaluation of the policy options". *Policy and Politics* 34(1), 91–113.

Williams, C. 2007. "Entrepreneurs operating in the informal economy: necessity or opportunity driven?". *Journal of Small Business and Entrepreneurship* 20(3), 309–20.

Williams, C. 2008. "Cross-national variations in undeclared work: results from a survey of 27 European countries". *International Journal of Economic Perspectives* 2(2), 46–63.

Williams, C. 2009. "Repaying favours: unravelling the nature of community exchange in an English locality". *Community Development Journal* 44(4), 488–99.

Williams, C. 2010a. "Beyond the formal/informal jobs divide: evaluating the prevalence of hybrid 'under–declared' employment in South-Eastern Europe". *International Journal of Human Resource Management* 21(14), 2529–46.

Williams, C. 2010b. "Spatial variations in the hidden enterprise culture: some lessons from England". *Entrepreneurship and Regional Development* 22(5), 403–23.

Williams, C. 2010c. "Re-theorizing the informal economy in western nations: some lessons from rural England". *Open Area Studies Journal* 3, 1–11.

Williams, C. 2012a. "Cross-national variations in the under-reporting of wages in South-East Europe: a result of over-regulation or under-regulation?". *South East European Journal of Economics and Business* 7(1), 53–61.

Williams, C. 2012b. "Explaining undeclared wage payments by employers in Central and Eastern Europe: a critique of the neo-liberal de-regulatory theory". *Debatte: Journal of Contemporary Central and Eastern Europe* 20(1), 3–20.

Williams, C. 2013a. "Beyond the formal economy: evaluating the level of employment in informal sector enterprises in global perspective". *Journal of Developmental Entrepreneurship* 18(4), 1–18.

Williams, C. 2013b. "Evaluating cross-national variations in the extent and nature of informal employment in the European Union". *Industrial Relations Journal* 44(5/6), 479–94.

Williams, C. 2013c. "Explaining employers' illicit envelope wage payments in the EU-27: a product of over- or under-regulation?". *Business Ethics: A European Review* 22(3), 325–40.

Williams, C. 2013d. "Evaluating the cross-national variations in under-declared wages in the European Union: an exploratory study". *Open Area Studies Journal* 5, 12–21.

Williams, C. 2014a. *Confronting the Shadow Economy: Evaluating Tax Compliance and Behaviour Policies*. Cheltenham: Elgar.

Williams, C. 2014b. "Out of the shadows: a classification of economies by the size and character of their informal sector". *Work, Employment and Society* 28(5), 735–53.

Williams, C. 2014c. "Explaining cross-national variations in the commonality of informal sector entrepreneurship: an exploratory analysis of 38 emerging economies". *Journal of Small Business and Entrepreneurship* 27(2), 191–212.

Williams, C. 2014d. "Public policy approaches towards the undeclared economy in European countries: a critical overview". *European Labour Law Journal* 5(2), 132–55.

Williams, C. 2015a. "Explaining cross-national variations in the informalisation of employment: some lessons from Central and Eastern Europe". *European Societies* 17(4), 492–512.

Williams, C. 2015b. "Explaining cross-national variations in the scale of informal employment: an exploratory analysis of 41 less developed economies". *International Journal of Manpower* 36(2), 118–35.

Williams, C. 2015c. "Entrepreneurship in the shadow economy: a review of the alternative policy approaches". *International Journal of Small and Medium Enterprises and Sustainability* 1(1), 51–82.

Williams, C. 2015d. "Out of the margins: classifying economies by the prevalence and character of employment in the informal economy". *International Labour Review* 154(3), 331–52.

Williams, C. 2016. *Diagnostic Report on Undeclared work in Greece*. Geneva: ILO.

Williams, C. 2017a. *Dependent Self-Employment in the European Union*. Geneva: ILO.

Williams, C. 2017b. *Developing a Holistic Approach for Tackling Undeclared Work: A Learning Resource*. Brussels: European Commission.

Williams, C. 2018. *Entrepreneurship in the Informal Sector: An Institutional Perspective*. Abingdon: Routledge.

Williams, C. & S. Bezeredi 2017. "Evaluating the use of personal connections to bypass formal procedures: a study of *vrski* in FYR Macedonia". *UTMS Journal of Economics* 8(2), 1–19.

Williams, C. & A. Gurtoo (eds) 2017a. *Routledge Handbook of Entrepreneurship in Developing Economies*. Abingdon: Routledge.

Williams, C. & A. Gurtoo 2017b. "The institutional environment of entrepreneurship in developing countries: an introductory overview". In C. Williams & A. Gurtoo (eds), *Routledge Handbook of Entrepreneurship in Developing Economies*, 13–16. Abingdon: Routledge.

Williams, C. & I. Horodnic 2015a. "Evaluating the prevalence of the undeclared economy in Central and Eastern Europe: an institutional asymmetry perspective". *European Journal of Industrial Relations* 21(4), 389–406.

Williams, C. & I. Horodnic 2015b. "Explaining and tackling the shadow economy in Estonia, Latvia and Lithuania: a tax morale approach". *Journal of Baltic Economics* 15(2), 81–98.

Williams, C. & I. Horodnic 2015c. "Explaining the prevalence of the informal economy in the Baltics: an institutional asymmetry perspective". *European Spatial Research and Policy* 22(2), 127–44.

Williams, C. & I. Horodnic 2016a. "Evaluating the illegal employer practice of under-reporting employees' salaries". *British Journal of Industrial Relations* 55(1), 83–111.

Williams, C. & I. Horodnic 2016b. "Cross-country variations in the participation of small businesses in the informal economy: an institutional asymmetry perspective". *Journal of Small Business and Enterprise Development* 23(1), 3–24.

Williams, C. & I. Horodnic 2016c. "An institutional theory of the informal economy: some lessons from the United Kingdom". *International Journal of Social Economics* 43(7), 722–38.

Williams, C. & I. Horodnic 2017. "Reconceptualising undeclared work as paid favours: implications for community economic development". *Community Development Journal* 53(4), 732–50.

Williams, C., I. Horodnic & J. Windebank 2015. "Explaining participation in the informal economy: an institutional incongruence perspective". *International Sociology* 30(3), 294–313.

Williams, C., I. Horodnic & J. Windebank 2017. "Evaluating the internal dualism of the informal sector: evidence from the European Union". *Journal of Economic Studies* 44(4), 605–16.

Williams, C. & A. Kedir 2016. "The impacts of corruption on firm performance: some lessons from 40 African countries". *Journal of Developmental Entrepreneurship* 21(4), 1–18.

Williams, C. & A. Kedir 2017a. "Starting-up unregistered and firm performance in Turkey". *International Entrepreneurship and Management Journal* 13(3), 797–817.

Williams, C. & A. Kedir 2017b. "Evaluating the impacts of starting-up unregistered on firm performance in Africa". *Journal of Developmental Entrepreneurship* 22(2), 1–17.

Williams, C. & A. Kedir 2018a. "Evaluating competing theories of informal sector entrepreneurship: a study of the determinants of cross-country variations in enterprises starting-up unregistered". *International Journal of Entrepreneurship and Innovation* 19(3), 155–65.

Williams, C. & A. Kedir 2018b. "Explaining cross-national variations in the prevalence of informal sector entrepreneurship: lessons from a survey of 142 countries". *Journal of Developmental Entrepreneurship* 23(1), 1–22.

Williams, C. & A. Kedir 2018c. "Explaining cross-country variations in the prevalence of informal sector competitors: lessons from the World Bank Enterprise Survey". *International Entrepreneurship and Management Journal.*

Williams, C. & B. Krasniqi 2018. "Explaining informal sector entrepreneurship in Kosovo: an institutionalist perspective". *Journal of Developmental Entrepreneurship* 23(2).

Williams, C. & M. Lansky 2013. "Informal employment in developed and emerging economies: perspectives and policy responses". *International Labour Review* 152(3/4), 355–80.

Williams, C. & F. Lapeyre 2017. *New Forms of Self-Employment: Trends, Challenges and Policy Responses in the EU.* Geneva: ILO.

Williams, C. & A. Martinez-Perez 2014a. "Do small business start-ups test-trade in the informal economy? Evidence from a UK small business survey". *International Journal of Entrepreneurship and Small Business* 22(1), 1–16.

Williams, C. & A. Martinez-Perez 2014b. "Is the informal economy an incubator for new enterprise creation? A gender perspective". *International Journal of Entrepreneurial Behaviour and Research* 20(1), 4–19.

Williams, C. & A. Martinez-Perez 2014c. "Why do consumers purchase goods and services in the informal economy?". *Journal of Business Research* 67(5), 802–06.

Williams, C. & A. Martinez-Perez 2014d. "Evaluating the cash-in-hand consumer culture in the European Union". *Journal of Contemporary European Studies* 22, 466–82.

Williams, C. & A. Martinez-Perez 2014e. "Entrepreneurship in the informal economy: a product of too much or too little state intervention?". *International Journal of Entrepreneurship and Innovation* 15(4), 227–37.

Williams, C. & A. Martinez-Perez 2016. "Evaluating the impacts of corruption on firm performance in developing economies: an institutional perspective". *International Journal of Business and Globalisation* 16(4), 401–22.

Williams, C., A. Martinez-Perez & A. Kedir 2016. "Does bribery have a negative impact on firm performance? A firm-level analysis across 132 developing countries". *International Journal of Entrepreneurial Behaviour and Research* 22(3), 398–415.

Williams, C., A. Martinez-Perez & A. Kedir 2017. "Informal entrepreneurship in developing economies: the impacts of starting-up unregistered on firm performance". *Entrepreneurship Theory and Practice* 41(5), 773–99.

Williams, C. & S. Nadin 2010. "Entrepreneurship and the informal economy: An overview". *Journal of Developmental Entrepreneurship* 15(4), 361–78.

Williams, C. & S. Nadin 2011a. "Evaluating the nature of the relationship between informal entrepreneurship and the formal economy in rural communities". *International Journal of Entrepreneurship and Innovation* 12(2), 95–103.

Williams, C. & S. Nadin 2011b. "Beyond a 'varieties of capitalism' approach in Central and Eastern Europe: some lessons from Ukraine". *Employee Relations* 33(4), 413–27.

Williams, C. & S. Nadin 2012a. "Tackling entrepreneurship in the informal economy: evaluating the policy options". *Journal of Entrepreneurship and Public Policy* 1(2), 111–24.

Williams, C. & S. Nadin 2012b. "Work beyond employment: representations of informal economic activities". *Work, Employment and Society* 26(2), 1–10.

Williams, C. & S. Nadin 2012c. "Tackling the hidden enterprise culture: government policies to support the formalization of informal entrepreneurship". *Entrepreneurship and Regional Development* 24(9/10), 895–915.

Williams, C. & S. Nadin 2013a. "Beyond the entrepreneur as a heroic figurehead of capitalism: re-representing the lived practices of entrepreneurs". *Entrepreneurship and Regional Development* 25(7/8), 552–68.

Williams, C. & S. Nadin 2013b. "Harnessing the hidden enterprise culture: supporting the formalization of off-the-books business start-ups". *Journal of Small Business and Enterprise Development* 20(2), 434–47.

Williams, C. & S. Nadin 2014. "Facilitating the formalisation of entrepreneurs in the informal economy: towards a variegated policy approach". *Journal of Entrepreneurship and Public Policy* 3(1), 33–48.

Williams, C., S. Nadin & M. Baric 2011. "Evaluating the participation of the self-employed in undeclared work: some evidence from a 27-nation European survey". *International Entrepreneurship and Management Journal* 7(3), 341–56.

Williams, C., S. Nadin & P. Rodgers 2012. "Evaluating competing theories of informal entrepreneurship: some lessons from Ukraine". *International Journal of Entrepreneurial Behaviour and Research* 18(5), 528–43.

Williams, C., S. Nadin & J. Windebank 2012. "Evaluating the prevalence and nature of self-employment in the informal economy: evidence from a 27-nation European survey". *European Spatial Research and Policy* 19(1), 129–42.

Williams, C. & O. Onoshchenko 2014. "Evaluating the role of *blat* in finding graduate employment in post-Soviet Ukraine: the 'dark side' of job recruitment?". *Employee Relations* 36(3), 254–65.

Williams, C. & O. Onoshchenko 2015. "An evaluation of the persistence of blat in post-Soviet societies: a case study of Ukraine's health services sector". *Studies in Transition States and Societies* 7(2), 46–63.

Williams, C. & P. Renooy 2013. *Tackling Undeclared Work in 27 European Union Member States and Norway: Approaches and Measures Since 2008*. Dublin: Eurofound.

Williams, C. & P. Renooy 2014. *Flexibility@Work 2014: Bringing the Undeclared Economy Out of the Shadows – the Role of Temporary Work Agencies*. Amsterdam: Randstad.

Williams, C. & J. Round 2007a. "Entrepreneurship and the informal economy: a study of Ukraine's hidden enterprise culture". *Journal of Developmental Entrepreneurship* 12(1), 119–36.

Williams, C. & J. Round 2007b. "Beyond negative depictions of informal employment: some lessons from Moscow". *Urban Studies* 44(12), 321–38.

Williams, C. & J. Round 2008. "The hidden enterprise culture of Moscow: entrepreneurship and off-the-books working practices". *Journal of Developmental Entrepreneurship* 13(4), 445–62.

Williams, C. & J. Round 2010. "Explaining participation in undeclared work: a result of exit or exclusion". *European Societies* 12(3), 391–418.

Williams, C., J. Round & P. Rodgers 2013. *The Role of Informal Economies in the Post-Soviet World: The End of Transition?* Abingdon: Routledge.

Williams, C. & F. Schneider 2016. *Measuring the Global Shadow Economy: The Prevalence of Informal Work and Labour.* Cheltenham: Elgar.

Williams, C. & M. Shahid 2016. "Informal entrepreneurship and institutional theory: explaining the varying degrees of (in)formalisation of entrepreneurs in Pakistan". *Entrepreneurship and Regional Development* 28(1/2), 1–25.

Williams, C., M. Shahid & A. Martinez 2016. "Determinants of the level of informality of informal micro-enterprises: some evidence from the city of Lahore, Pakistan". *World Development* 84, 312–25.

Williams, C. & J. Windebank 1998. *Informal Employment in the Advanced Economies: Implications for Work and Welfare.* London: Routledge.

Williams, C. & J. Windebank 1999. "The formalisation of work thesis: a critical evaluation". *Futures* 31(6), 547–58.

Williams, C. & J. Windebank 2001. "Reconceptualising paid informal exchange: some lessons from English cities". *Environment and Planning A*, 33(1), 121–40.

Williams, C. & J. Yang 2017. "Evaluating the use of personal networks to circumvent formal processes: a case study of *vruzki* in Bulgaria". *South East European Journal of Economics and Business* 12(1), 57–67.

Williams, C. *et al.* 2012a. *Enabling Enterprise: Tackling the Barriers to Formalisation.* London: Community Links.

Williams, C. *et al.* 2012b. "Evaluating 'varieties of capitalism' by the extent and nature of the informal economy: the case of South-Eastern Europe". *South Eastern Europe Journal of Economics* 10(2), 87–104.

Williams, C. *et al.* 2018. *An Evaluation of the Scale of Undeclared Work in the European Union and its Structural Determinants: Estimates Using the Labour Input Method.* Brussels: European Commission.

Windebank, J. & I. Horodnic 2017. "Explaining participation in undeclared work in France: lessons for policy evaluation". *International Journal of Sociology and Social Policy* 37(3/4), 203–17.

Woodruff, C., S. de Mel & D. Mckenzie 2013. "The demand for, and consequences of, formalization among informal firms in Sri Lanka". *Applied Economics* 5(2), 122–50.

Woolfson, C. 2007. "Pushing the envelope: the 'informalization' of labour in post-communist new EU member states". *Work, Employment and Society* 21(5), 551–64.

World Bank 2013. *World Development Indicators.* Washington, DC: World Bank. Available at: http://data.worldbank.org/data–catalog/world–development–indicators (accessed 10 January 2018).

Wunsch-Vincent, S., J. de Beer & K. Fu 2015. "What we know and do not know about innovation in the informal economy". In E. Kraemer-Mbula & S. Wunsch-Vincent (eds), *The Informal Economy in Developing Nations: Hidden Engine of Innovation?*, 142–60. Cambridge: Cambridge University Press.

Yamada, G. 1996. "Urban informal employment and self-employment in developing countries: theory and evidence". *Economic Development and Cultural Change* 44(2), 244–66.

Yusuff, O. 2011. "A theoretical analysis of the concept of informal economy and informality in developing countries". *European Journal of Social Sciences* 20(4), 624–36.

Žabko, O. & F. Rajevska 2007. "Undeclared work and tax evasion: case of Latvia". Paper presented at colloquium of the Belgian Federal Service for Social Security on Undeclared Work, Tax Evasion and Avoidance, Brussels.

Zelizer, V. 2005. *The Purchase of Intimacy*. Princeton, NJ: Princeton University Press.

Index

Note: bold page numbers indicate tables; italic page numbers indicate figures.